AMERICA THE FINAL DESTINATION

AMERICA THE FINAL DESTINATION

OR
THE NEW WORLD (LOVE STORY)

REA-SILVIA COSTIN, P.E.

Author's Disclaimer: Any resemblance between the personages of this book and real persons is purely coincidental.

Table of Contents

INTRODUCTION

This book is the third book of a trilogy that spans the life of three generations of strong women: Calliope, the author's grandmother; Thiana, the author's mother; and the author herself, Silver.

7iana: AVDELA-A Macedonian Village in the Northwestern Greece depicts Calliope and Thiana's lives. The action takes place in a small village in northwestern Greece—AVDELA, moves to Thesalonika, and later to Bucharest Romania, where Thiana married and established. The book encompasses the 1920s to the 1970s, including events associated with World War 2 and the rise of the Iron Curtain that separated eastern Europe for the rest of the world.

Athens, the second book of the trilogy, follows Silver's adventures after she defected from communist Romania to live in Greece.

Love Story (7e New World), the third book of the trilogy, follows Silver as she arrives in a new country— America—and starts a new life.

Love Story (7e New World) is a beautiful romance in which Silver falls in love with her new country, with Florida, and Matthew.

FIRST LOVE

This story is dedicated to my father, Stefan Costin, who taught me the love of books and the dedication to study.

God's Mansion

I'll never get back there.
I'll never set foot inside that house.
Somebody else has it now.
The high ceilings, the paint and moldings
Different colors in each room,
Green, blue, beige, and red
Matching the tall ceramic stove's colors
The sun filtering through heavy velvet drapes
Different colors in each room
Matching the antiques ceramic stove
The gleaming of the hard wood floor
The tall white doors with intricate moldings on top
Painted different colors in each room
Matching the corner ceramic stoves
The feeling that I'm home
"You're home," the voice at the end of the tunnel said
"God has a mansion for you in heaven"
"You're home now!"

CHAPTER 1

The Arrival

Silver remembered the night she arrived in the United States, almost exactly two years ago. It had been a long, nine-hour flight from Greece to Rome and on to the John F. Kennedy Airport in New York. She'd brought a lot of luggage with her, her entire fortune, everything she had accumulated while living in Greece, and whatever her mother had sent her from Romania—all her belongings.

It was more than what most of the other refugees had. Other Romanian immigrants were on the airplane going to various destinations in the United States to be with their respective sponsors. The airplane was practically full of Romanian refugees, all speaking loudly amongst themselves, smoking, laughing nervously— anything to disguise their fear of unknown, their anxiety.

It was the first time since they'd left home that they were treated politely and with respect, like human beings. The stewardesses asked them nicely what they would like to eat from the menu and this courtesy was so different from the situations and places each of them had come from.

"What would you like to have for dinner?" The stewardess hovered above Silver.

"What is on the menu?" Silver asked. The stewardess was different than all the women she knew. She wore a lot of make-up. Her cheeks were too red and the metallic blue eye shadow made her look older than she was.

"We have two choices, lasagna or chicken. What would you like?" "The lasagna, please. I've never had it before."

"What did you choose?" the boy sitting next to her asked. He wore headphones and was listening to music.

Silver would have liked to listen to the music, too, but she understood that there was a small fee, and she did not want to deplete her small reserve of money.

"The lasagna," Silver said.

"I'll try that too. Would you like to listen to the music?" the boy asked. He was maybe eighteen, twenty years old.

"Yes, but I don't want to spend the money for it."

"Listen, I will pay for you. While I stayed in Athens, waiting to come to America, I worked for a man with a computer shop. I set up his computer. I learned how back in Romania, in school. He gave me $500.00 when I left."

"That's a lot of money. It will help you and your parents get established in America."

"We are going to stay with relatives in Orlando, Florida. They've already rented an apartment for us. Have you heard about Orlando?"

"No."

"It is in the center of Florida. It is where Disney World is located." "Is that so? Of course I've heard about Disney World."

"I'm going to work with computers. I heard that they need specialists in computers in America."

Silver knew she was going to stay with her uncle, her mother's first cousin, who lived near New York, in Manhasset. While still in Greece, she wrote to him, and he wrote a nice letter back.

She relaxed, put her headphones on, and slept.

When the airplane arrived in New York, representatives of the World Council of Churches, who facilitated her departure from Greece to the United States, awaited the new lot of refugees, calling everyone by name and number. Silver was among the last ones to be accounted for. The young girl who called her name greeted her, welcomed her to the United States and her new life here, and handed her an airplane ticket to Jacksonville, Florida, informing her that she'd better move quickly because the airplane to Jacksonville, connecting through Atlanta, was departing within minutes from a different gate.

Silver was astonished.

"Look, this has to be a mistake," Silver said to the girl. "I am supposed to stay in New York. My uncle has the papers to sponsor me! I am supposed to stay here."

"I only know what I am supposed to tell you. Your sponsor, the people who applied to sponsor you here in America, are from Jacksonville, not New York," the girl answered in a rush. "Take your airplane ticket for Jacksonville. And hurry. The airplane to Atlanta leaves in twenty minutes from a different gate. Ask the flight attendant at the desk which gate you have to go to. Excuse me, I have to attend to those other people. They don't speak any English."

The girl turned her back and left Silver standing in the middle of the hallway with her luggage gathered around her feet.

"Would you please tell me where I have to go for the airplane to Atlanta?" Silver asked the flight attendant at the desk. "What is going to happen with my luggage from the cargo of the plane?"

"You have to go to gate twelve down the hallway with your carry-on luggage," the man behind the desk responded politely. "Don't worry about your luggage. It will be automatically forwarded to your plane; you don't have to worry about it."

"I have to change planes in Atlanta and take another flight to Jacksonville, Florida; that's what they're telling me, now. But I don't know how to change airplanes by myself. It is my first time in the United States. I am a refugee. Who is going to take care of me in Atlanta?"

"Calm down! The attendants in Atlanta can tell you which gate to go to. You won't need any special help. You'll know what to do. Look at you! You don't look like a refugee! You are better dressed than we Americans, and you speak good English. Certainly you are not shy. You will be just fine!"

They gave her a cart to haul her luggage and she rushed to the departure gate for Atlanta.

* * *

Silver had totally forgotten about her brief meeting with Kiki in her uncle's shop in Athens; they'd met the past summer when Kiki was visiting Greece and she had promised to sponsor her. Silver remembered the strange-looking woman she'd met in her uncle's shop. She was in her mid-thirties, was very tan, and wore tight short shorts, like all tourists. Her uncle, Vanghely, told her that Kiki used to work in his shop before she married an American man and left with him. Kiki had mentioned that she'd sponsor Silver, but then she'd paid no attention to her, even though Kiki asked for her personal data and took notes on a small notepad that she kept in her oversize purse.

* * *

Silver knew she looked her best. She'd tried to dress appropriately for her new life when she left Athens ten hours ago. She was wearing her gray velvet Italian jeans and the thin, pink blouse she bought for herself in Athens with a white wool coat draped over her shoulders.

She'd started to learn English a year before she left her native country, Romania, taking night classes at the University. During the year she stayed in Greece, preparing to come the USA, she attended English classes at the Hellenic-American Institute in Athens.

* * *

It was late, and she was tired after too many hours of flying, but she couldn't dare relax. The hard part was just beginning. When she arrived at the airport in Atlanta, Silver understood she was in a new country. The airport in New York had been different, with crowds of people rushing in different directions; its old style reminded her of the airports and the train stations in Europe. Atlanta was totally different. The people were nice and courteous; the place was neat and clean, and everything looked very organized with plenty of open space. It was a scene different from everything she'd known and seen until that moment. She liked it.

She explained her situation to the flight attendant on the flight, and when they arrived, the airline staff provided her with an automatic carrier and took her and her luggage to the departure gate for Jacksonville. Everything ran smoothly and efficiently.

Finally, she arrived in Jacksonville. It was probably 2:00 a.m. She looked around. The Jacksonville airport was in no way as modern as the one in Atlanta, but she found her luggage on the rotating conveyer belt, and looked around for someone to recognize and claim her. She saw Kiki and her husband, whom she did not know, waiting on a bench to pick her up.

"Silvia, Hi! I'm Kiki! Do you remember me? We met in Vanghely's shop in Athens this summer."

"Of course I remember you! Thank you for following through with the sponsorship papers for me!"

"Silver, this is my husband Steven!"

"Hi! Nice to meet you." Silver looked over the tall, skinny man. He looked like he was in his early forties, Silver thought.

They made a strange pair, Kiki short and small and her husband very tall.

With no further discussion, Kiki's husband placed all her luggage in his big, oversized car, and they drove for what Silver thought to be the longest drive in her life.

On the way to Jacksonville Beach, she saw wide, empty roads, huge overhead signs, dim lights, and long, long stretches of highway.

When they finally arrived, Kiki's house was nice—it was comfortable, large, and very well kept. Carefully trimmed bushes formed a nice flowery hedge against the house; the thick green grass had been perfectly manicured. Inside, the house was spacious with its large living room/kitchen area and high vaulted ceiling.

They had prepared a bedroom for Silver and she was shown the adjacent bathroom that she was to use. Shortly, with not much fuss, everybody went to bed. Kiki's husband was to go to work the next morning. Finally, Silver found herself alone in her bedroom.

She allowed herself to think about what was happening to her and what course her life was taking. In the tiny white bedroom that belonged to one of Kiki's daughters, the full realization of what had happened to her became clear. Until this moment, she'd blocked all thought of what was going to happen to her in her new country. There, in the dark, she knew she was truly alone. She'd been cut off from her roots, from her family and friends, from everyone she knew; she was suddenly alone in the world, and she became frightened. It was like she was the only human being on Earth with no connections to anyone. Never before in her life had she been afraid, but now fear took hold of her. She could not sleep.

Finally, dawn came and with it the first signs of light. In the distance she could hear what sounded like a factory or a power plant. Familiar sounds. Construction work. She was not alone after all. People were working here like they worked back in Romania or Greece.

CHAPTER 2

Kiki

Kiki's family woke up and began to prepare for the day. Silver could hear noises and hushed voices outside her bedroom door. The daughters used the next-door bathroom to get ready for school. Kiki's husband left for work. The school bus stopped for the girls. Familiar things.

Silver thought that life was the same regardless of the country: people are the same everywhere, going about their lives, their work.

When the house quieted down, Silver rose from her bed, took her bathrobe and towel, and went into the adjacent bathroom. The bathroom was spotless, done in shades of pink with pink ribbons tying back the sheer, white bathtub curtains. Silver ran a hot bath and soaked for a good while. The long journey had left her bone-tired.

Once she was done with her bath, she went into the kitchen. Wonderful smells wafted from the kitchen: fresh coffee, vanilla, and bacon.

Kiki had taken the day off from work to spend it with her. Silver poured herself a mug of hot, black coffee. She watched as Kiki made French toast in a black-bottom, non-stick frying pan and removed crispy strips of bacon from the microwave.

They had breakfast at the round oak table in the modern kitchen that Kiki's husband had remodeled. The kitchen had a stained-glass ceiling which reflected the soft light through panes of glass of various colors and designs. There was an immaculate glass-top stove, electric oven and microwave, and a multitude of electric gadgets that Silver had never seen before.

"How is Vanghely?" Kiki asked in her broken English.

"He is fine. He works in the shop all day. How did you come to know him?"

"When I was thirteen years old, I worked for him in the shop. My family, my parents, brothers and sisters are still there, in Athens."

"What made you come to America?"

"I met my husband when he was stationed in Greece with the Navy. We dated and he proposed to me. I am very lucky; I have a very good husband. Other Greek girls, some of my friends, are not so lucky. They have Greek husbands and they are not so good."

"Why? What is wrong with Greek men?"

"They fool around with other women, and they expect you to work like a slave."

"How long have you lived here?"

"Seventeen years now. Tina, my oldest daughter, is sixteen and Kula, my youngest, is fourteen."

"Do you like it here? Don't you miss Greece and your family?"

"I have everything I need. Back in Greece my family is very poor. Here, I have this beautiful house and a pool and two cars and jewelry, everything I want."

"Where do you work?"

"I'm a waitress at a restaurant. I work very hard, but I make good money. Some of my friends, Greek girls, do not work and they envy me for what I have."

Later, they got dressed and left in Kiki's car, a huge white Lincoln Eldorado with a plush red interior. Their first stop was at the Social Security office. Silver needed a Social Security number to be able to work. The Social Services office was located downtown on the second floor of the Federal building. The room was crowded with people seated on rows of blue chairs, patiently waiting for their turn to be called by the worker seated behind a small window. Silver filled out the necessary paperwork and received her Social Security number right away.

Next, Kiki took Silver to visit some of her friends: Greek girls married to American Navy men like her. First, they visited Maria, who was a belly dancer in a Greek restaurant. They stopped in front of a small house built out of concrete blocks in a crowded neighborhood— Arlington, as Kiki called it. They rang the bell and a young woman in her thirties opened the door and greeted Kiki. She was beautiful, with long flowing black hair and black eyes.

"Come inside please. I was just sewing curtains for my boys' bedroom," Maria said.

"This is Silver. I told you about her. She is from Greece. She'll be staying here," Kiki said. "Maria is a belly dancer. And she is married to my husband's friend from the Navy."

"That is not entirely true. I hadn't been dancing for a long time, actually since I came here to the United States, really. But, now that my friend has a Greek restaurant, he's asked me to dance evenings. I am just getting back in shape. It's really hard and my belly really hurts. I have not used those muscles in a long time."

"How are the curtains coming along?"

"Very well." Lengths of material were stretched over the entire living room floor.

"We don't want to interrupt you from your work. We just stopped by to say hello." Kiki excused herself, and they were on their way to visit the other Maria, a Greek girl married to a Greek man who owned the restaurant where Maria was a belly dancer.

Maria worked hard from dawn to night in the restaurant's kitchen while her husband served as the host. Not hard work for him, surely, Kiki informed her in the car.

Maria was a young girl of maybe twenty-five, but she'd aged prematurely because of all the hard work she'd done. Her face looked pale, unhealthy, and she had a big scar at the base of her neck. She'd had her thyroid gland removed, Silver thought.

They sat in the restaurant's kitchen, a long dark room crowded with stoves, refrigerators, and pots and pans of all shapes.

"I just want to go back to Greece and at least be close to my family," Maria said in Greek.

"Don't you know any English?" Silver asked.

"No. With whom would I speak English? I wake up every morning at five and start kneading dough for the pizzas. Then I wash the kitchen and start preparing the food for lunch."

"Don't you talk to the customers?

"I only work in the kitchen. My husband hired some nice young girls who speak English as waitresses."

"Doesn't your husband help you at all?"

"No! He hangs out at a table in the restaurant every evening and drinks with his friends and the customers. Then, we go home and I have the little baby to feed and take care of."

"Where is the baby during the day?" Silver wanted to know everything.

"He stays at a day care center during the day. I can't take care of him here in the kitchen. I take him home evenings and my husband drops him at day care in the morning after he gets him up."

"Is the restaurant making good money?"

"No. We intend to sell it and move back to Greece. At least there I have my family to help me."

"We are moving back to Greece pretty soon, too," Kiki announced. "In maybe ten days my husband completes his twenty-year service commitment with the Navy, and we plan to sell the house and move back to Greece."

"Are you going to move my things with yours?" Maria asked. "Yes. Start packing whatever you want to take back with you. The Navy is paying for the last move. They will pay for the shipping of my furniture to Greece. So pack what you want and the movers will pick it up with my things."

"But what are you going to do with the girls? Aren't they still in school?" Silver asked incredulously. She felt her heart sink. She just arrived and felt relatively safe with Kiki and her family. What was she supposed to do when Kiki left?

"They are almost through with school," Kiki answered. "They have to get married. I married when I was their age."

"And what will happen with me, then?"

"You probably need to get married too."

"When exactly do you intend to move?" Silver asked.

"As soon as the house sells. I put it on the market with Watson Realtors. It will sell quickly."

CHAPTER 3

Job-Hunting

From that moment on, Silver's life began to spin at a fast pace. Looking back, she could not believe how much had happened in the span of just ten days.

"I was thinking you could take a job as a housekeeper with a nice family here in Jacksonville," Kiki said.

"Housekeeper? I am an Engineer, Kiki. I am highly trained."

"Just until you get your feet on the ground. A lot of young girls—students—are housekeepers while they finish their schooling."

"I am not going to school; I've finished my education. I know everything there is to know about engineering," Silver said.

She had not left Romania to be a housekeeper in America. That was not why she'd gone to college and earned her Master's Degree in Engineering. That was not why she'd studied so hard for so many years, passed so many exams.

As much as she admired Kiki for her practical ways and the nice life she provided for her children and the nice house she owned, housekeeping was *not* what Silver wanted for herself.

It was the intellectual challenge, the freedom of spirit she was after, even if it meant a hardship to start with. She wanted to practice what she knew, what she knew she was good at, what she loved passionately—her profession. Silver often thought that her profession was her first love. She spared no effort, no amount of time, when it came to studying, or doing her job right. Work was an outlet to express her creativity and talent and that was as essential as breath itself for Silver.

Silver felt trapped. She felt as if she was drowning and she had to reach deep within herself to use the inner, hidden, resources she possessed and start fighting for what she thought was right for her, for what she wanted out of life.

Every day, Kiki and her husband left the house early in the morning and returned home after dark. The girls left for school in the morning by bus, and returned home around three o'clock. Then they fixed something light to eat for themselves, watched television for a few hours, talked over the phone with their friends, and went to bed, or at least to their rooms around seven o'clock. Silver went to her room at the same time.

Silver was trapped in the house all day with no means of transportation or communication with the outside world.

Finally, late one evening, she waited for Kiki's husband to return from work. He was a supervisor at a sewage treatment plant, and the Navy was sending him to classes after work. When he got home, usually around nine or nine-thirty at night, he was exhausted; his eyes were red and he barely had energy left to eat a light supper with his wife and go to bed.

That evening, Silver waited for Steve. She took her Construction Engineering textbook out of her luggage, the one she had brought from Romania, which encompassed all she knew about Engineering, and showed it to Kiki's husband after he finished eating. He leafed through it.

"Do you really know how to do all this?" he asked, incredulously. "Yes, I do," Silver answered. "Better said, I know how to design projects. I am in the design, not the construction end of engineering." "I can see from these pictures the dams used for water supply. The Army Corps of Engineers has them built all over the country."

"I know how to design them. As a matter of fact, I designed several of them back in Romania."

"If indeed what you say if true, if you know what's in this book, you'll easily be able to find a job here," he said.

The next evening, he brought Silver the local newspaper and showed her how to look at the classified ads for jobs; he showed her where to look under the ads for technical jobs.

Silver now had something to go by, a point of reference to start her search. She found an ad about a local company in need of an engineer and called for an interview. The company's secretary arranged an interview for the next day.

Silver asked Kiki if she could drive her to the interview.

"Let me see the address," Kiki answered. "You know, I don't drive downtown. It's too dangerous. I only drive back and forth to my job here on Beach Boulevard, and maybe to the grocery story nearby. Steve drives us everywhere else."

Silver showed her the company's name and address.

"It's in Arlington. Maybe I can drive you there, but you'll have to come with me to my job in the morning and wait until I can take you over."

* * *

The next morning, Silver dressed professionally in a pantsuit she'd brought from Greece, and left with Kiki around five o'clock in the morning.

Kiki worked at The Pancake House on Beach Boulevard. The restaurant was famous for its breakfasts. People on their way to work stopped to have a hearty breakfast of pancakes with maple syrup, eggs, bacon, and hot coffee or orange juice. Kiki set the tables, cleaned, took orders, and served the food, all with a smile and a cheerful attitude. She knew everybody by name and greeted them and exchanged jokes. In return, customers left her big tips.

Around ten o'clock the place quieted down. The waitresses took breaks from their hard work, talking among themselves and eating breakfast. Kiki brought Silver toast and coffee to a table in the back, and they sat down to eat.

It was time to go for the dreaded interview. Kiki was dressed in her waitress uniform: a short orange dress. She navigated the big car cautiously, and they arrived at a small office building in Arlington.

"I am here for the job opening. I called yesterday. Do you remember me? My name is Silver."

"You have such a lovely accent. Where are you from?" "I am from Romania. I have an interview at 11:30."

"Fill out this application first. Sit over there at that desk and take your time."

Silver had to describe the type of work she was familiar with. She returned the application and waited for the company's owner to look it over.

"Please came to my office." A small, nearly bald man approached with his hand stretched out toward Silver. "I am Mr. Libentag, the company's owner."

They entered a small office cluttered with drawings and papers. "I've looked over your application carefully. You have an impressive background. You will find a job. But my company specializes in mechanical engineering. You're more of a civil engineer, according to the type of work you mentioned here. Here, I made a list of the companies in town where you might find employment."

Back at home, Silver took the telephone directory, confirmed the companies' names, addresses, and telephone numbers, and started to call the offices. She first explained to the receptionists who she was and what her situation was, and requested that they mail her applications. Everybody was nice and polite and sympathetic.

Soon she started receiving applications by mail. She filled them out and mailed them back.

Meanwhile, she found another position advertised in the newspaper for a city job. Kiki took her again for an interview in the city of Jacksonville. City hall was a tall building downtown right on the river. The Personnel Director, a tall black man, looked over the application she'd filled out.

"The City's position is for an engineering aid. According to your qualifications you should try for an engineering position and not an engineering aid position. We do not have an opening right now."

"I would take the engineering aid position, just to get started," Silver said hopefully. "What are the job requirements?"

"The job is for somebody with a high school diploma, nothing more, to help the engineers do their jobs"

"I'll take it," Silver exclaimed.

"No. We cannot hire people overqualified for the position. It's against the law. You will find something better with your qualifications."

CHAPTER 4

Job-Hunting II

Wednesdays were Kiki's free days. She worked Saturdays, but was given Wednesdays off. On Saturdays, Kiki's husband, Steve, woke up early in the morning and cooked for the girls and for Silver. He took out the heavy skillet and fried eggs and bacon. Next, he did the laundry. Everybody, Silver included, stacked their dirty clothes in a sack in the garage, and on Saturday Steve did the laundry. He carefully separated the whites and the colored clothes, the fine blouses and dresses. Then, with Tina's help, he vacuumed the house from one end to the other. Silver did her share of household chores. She washed dishes and cleaned the kitchen.

Later, when Kiki got home from her job, the entire family went to Morison's, a nearby cafeteria, for a nice meal.

The next Wednesday, Kiki took Silver to the local Lutheran Social Services where they had people who specialized in finding jobs for immigrants and helping them with their resumes.

From then on, Silver's path became clear. She enrolled in English classes offered by Lutheran Social Services at the main library downtown. She learned to take the bus from Kiki's house to go downtown for classes.

"Do you speak Romanian?" Silver asked the beautiful, young girl at the Lutheran Social Services office.

"Yes. I am Romanian. Or better said, I came from Romania ten years ago. Now, I am an American," the young girl answered in Romanian. "By the way, my name is Rodica."

She was in her twenties, with short hair and wore a white nurse's uniform.

"I'm Silver. I just arrived from Romania via Greece. Do you work here?" Silver asked.

"No, I'm a nurse at the University Hospital downtown. I only work here on a volunteer basis whenever they need me. I help with translation. They called me because of this guy, Silviu, who came here from New York by bus. They cannot figure out what is going on with him. He's in pretty bad shape. He had some bad experiences in New York, and he is in a state of shock. They couldn't find anybody else who could talk to him."

"How awful. Where is he now?"

"I knew this gentleman, Mr. Joca, a friend of mine. He's a counselor at the Florida Junior College here. Mr. Joca took him in to his house on the beach. He is of Romanian heritage even though he doesn't speak any Romanian."

"I need to translate my diploma, and to put together a resume. Can you help me with it?"

"I'll help you with the translation. Also I'll introduce you to Mr. Joca. He'll help you with your résumé." "That'll be fine."

"I have to go now. Would you like to come by my house? I can help you with the translation and maybe I'll show you around town."

"That would be wonderful!"

"I'll come and pick you up at your house tomorrow afternoon at five o'clock," Rodica said.

* * *

The next day, Rodica came by Kiki's house. She drove a big new car—a beige Lincoln Continental.

They went to Rodica's house in Arlington.

The house, located in an older section of town, was quite small and made from concrete blocks. Inside, the house was nicely furnished and sparkling clean. Silver could recognize the few porcelain figurines and red crystal vases as Romanian-made.

"This is Silver. My husband, Joe," Rodica made the introductions. "Rodi told me about you. Welcome to America." The young slender

man seemed pleasant. He had a full head of thick brown hair, and a bushy beard and eyebrows. He wore glasses.

"Do you speak any Romanian?" Silver asked.

"No. I was born here. Rodi's mother doesn't speak any English. Here, we are in America. We need to speak English." "What do you do?"

"I'm an engineering student."

"That's quite a coincidence. I am an engineer, too. Where do you go to school?"

"I'm taking classes at Jacksonville University. Later on I'll go to South Florida to finish."

"I want to show Silver the mall. She has to know where to shop in case she needs something."

"O.K., you two. Go and have fun. No speaking in Romanian, Rodi.

Silver needs to practice her English."

The mall proved to be an exciting experience for Silver. Miles upon miles of indoor shops. They walked the seven miles of shops until Silver couldn't feel her feet. Finally, they sat down at an ice cream parlor for a treat.

"Are you going to go to class tomorrow?" Rodica asked. "I'm planning to."

"Good. I'll come at lunch and pick you up at the Library. We're going to visit Mr. Joca at Florida Junior College."

* * *

The next day, Rodica came and picked Silver up at the Main Street library and they both went to the Florida Junior College downtown.

"Rodi, what a pleasure to see you." Mr. Joca came forward to meet them in the lobby and conducted them back to his office. He was an elderly gentleman with a slight stutter.

"This is Silver," Rodi said. "I told you about her." "Nice to meet you." "How is Silviu doing?" Silver wanted to know.

"He is much better. He is such a smart young man. We are learning English together. What a shame he had such a bad experience back in New York."

"What happened to him?" Silver asked.

"Some people, Romanians, took advantage of him. He is fine now. I asked him to make lists of English words he learns every day. He is teaching me Romanian and I'm teaching him English."

"I'm glad to hear he is feeling better," Silver said. "Rodi told me that you could help me put together my resume."

"I will be glad to. If you have some time now, you can sit down and put down in your own words what you did back in Romania and then, we will try to make some sense out of it."

"Thanks a lot. Yes, I have the time if you do."

"I'll leave the two of you then. I need to get back to my job." Rodi turned to leave the office.

"Rodi, let's plan to get together some time soon. You know Betty is happy to see you and Joe. We'll have a boiled shrimp and peanuts party pretty soon."

Mr. Joca helped Silver with her resume.

* * *

Social Services announced that there was an opening at the state office which might be of interest for Silver.

Silver talked with a woman at Social Services. The woman, a beautiful young black woman, gave her the most precious advice of all, "Everything they ask: if you know how to do it, your answer is, I can! Later on, after you get the job and put your feet on the ground, they will teach you how to do the very same thing they were asking about." Silver translated her diploma with Mr. Joca's help, and Rodica's help, and with the resume and a copy of the translation of her credentials, she went for the interview at the state office.

Silver dressed very carefully for the interview. She put on her sheer Romanian blouse with beige crochet inserts, and a freshly-starched, yellow cotton skirt that was very stylish. She matched it with beige, high-heeled sandals. She looked cool, dressed for the hot weather in Jacksonville.

Kiki again drove her to the interview and waited in the car.

Silver entered the building and announced to the secretary that she had an interview scheduled with the head of the engineering division for the newly advertised position.

After a while, the Chief Engineer, a small, older man, came over. "I'm Mr. Watkins, Frank Watkins. I'm the lead engineer here. Please come into the conference room and let's talk a little." He showed Silver a plan, a blue print. "Please describe in your own words exactly what you see on this plan?"

"It's a plan for a residential development and stormwater pond," Silver answered, almost instantly. "The pond is for the treatment of runoff before it enters the creek."

"Do you have any experience with the design of storm water systems?"

"Yes, that's my specialty. I finished the Faculty of Hydrotechnical Constructions in Bucharest, Romania."

"And do you have hands on experience with design?"

"Yes, I worked before I came here as a design engineer for a company in Romania and also while I lived in Greece."

The boss seemed impressed with her self-assurance, with the fact that she did not hesitate before answering, and also with her command of the English language. Of course she had a strong accent, that probably would stay with her for the rest of her life, but she could communicate clearly in English. He took her resume and the translation of her diploma and her credentials, a summary of all classes she took in college, and went to talk to his boss, the Director of the state office, while Silver waited in the conference room.

After a while, he came back and took Silver to the Director's office to introduce her. The Director looked like a nice man. He shook Silver's hand and welcomed her to her new country, America. "I am impressed by your command of the English Language. Frank tells me that you have good working experience in storm-water design."

"Thank you. I understand everything and can communicate what I want clearly, I hope. And, yes, I have experience in storm-water design"

"I am impressed. We will contact you."

* * *

Meanwhile, Kiki was going ahead with her plans to sell the house. She put it on the market with Watson Real Estate, and people started to come and look at the house with the real estate agent. Silver, who was home most of the time, opened the door and let them in and remained quiet while the real estate agent showed the house.

The house was a good buy with the improvements Kiki's husband had made to it, and it sold quickly. Kiki and her husband agreed to withhold the second mortgage and the sale came through within a few days.

The Navy was paying for the last move for Kiki's husband, and Kiki, always the practical woman, took advantage and bought things for her relatives in Greece.

The moving company contracted by the Navy came and carefully packed the entire household, the furniture, and everything else Kiki bought to take with them in Greece.

Something had to be done about Silver. She needed a house to stay in until she got her feet on the ground and could survive on her own.

CHAPTER 5

Maria

"Listen, I know a Greek lady, Maria. She comes to the restaurant from time to time. She is a real lady. I would like for you to meet her. She said she would like to meet you, too. I'll take you with me tomorrow. Be sure you dress nicely," Kiki said as soon as she entered the house that evening.

The next day, Silver dressed up in a gray linen pantsuit she'd brought from Greece, and she left with Kiki at five o'clock in the morning.

Kiki was busy setting up the tables, brewing coffee, and serving the first customers who started to show up as early as six-thirty to have breakfast. They were hard working men: truck drivers and laborers who were on their way to a long day's work. Kiki moved fast between the tables, back and forth from the kitchen carrying trays and plates full of food, pots of fresh coffee, and mugs full of orange and grapefruit juice. She happily joked with the customers.

The first rush was over by eight-thirty. Silver waited at a table in the back.

Finally around nine, a well-dressed lady with short gray hair entered the restaurant. She took a table next to a window, and Silver noticed Kiki rush to her side. She brought Silver to meet her.

"Maria, this is the girl I mentioned to you, Silver," Kiki said. "Kiki mentioned that you are from Romania and your mother is Greek. Do you speak Greek?"

"A little. Not grammatically correct, but I lived in Greece for a year before I came here."

"My father came from Greece many years ago. He entered America through Ellis Island. We are all immigrants here in America. We all started that way. Are you going to church?"

"Back in Romania religion was forbidden by the Communist regime. But, yes, I was baptized Christian Orthodox. We went every year, even back in Romania, to Church for Easter. In Greece, I went to the Church more often."

"I will take you with me to the Greek Orthodox Church here in Jacksonville this coming Sunday. Would you like that?"

"Yes, very much so."

"Kiki was telling me that you will need a place to live after she moves."

"That's right."

"I think I know a girl, a nurse with the Navy, who would be interested. She is looking for a roommate. Her name is Peggy and she's about your age."

"That sounds great."

Silver never knew for sure what had been said or exactly why Maria took an interest in her. Maybe it had something to do with her Greek heritage and also, perhaps with the fact that southern people were more hospitable than the ones living up north. Being an immigrant was not considered something to be ashamed of.

The next Sunday morning, Maria came to Kiki's house to take Silver to the Greek church in town. Maria came inside. Maria's hair was perfectly groomed. Diamond studs shone in her earlobes. She wore a heavy silk dress, dark blue with small white dots. Her face was perfectly made-up.

"This is my daughter, Carol," Maria introduced Silver to a young, beautiful girl waiting outside in the car. Maria drove a white Mercedes. Silver liked Maria very much. She was smooth talking and elegantly dressed and she took a real interest in Silver. She listened to Silver's story and concerns, her hopes, and desires.

Maria drove the car smoothly and soon they arrived in front of a monumental building located on Atlantic Boulevard, not far from downtown.

"This is the St. John the Divine Greek Orthodox Church," Maria said.

"It looks like the Acropolis," Silver said. "Not quite, of course, but the general idea, the first impression." The flight of stairs leading up to the building, with arched entrance and cupola, all reminded her of Greece.

"It is the work of a local Greek architect," Maria said.

The inside of the church was a little different from the churches she'd visited back in Romania and in Greece. More modern, more stylized, but the same feeling, same peace—God's peace. Light filtered through small windows artfully placed next to the ceiling in the walls. The huge windows were stained glass scenes of various saints. Same feeling. The House of God.

They took their seats on the neatly arranged blue cushioned benches. Silver peered around at the Greek-American people filling the church. The priest wore the heavily ornate robes, as did the priests in Romania and Greece. He gave the sermon in English and in Greek.

After the service, they stopped for coffee and sweets in a large room in the basement of the church. Maria introduced her to Father Costopulos, the Greek priest.

"Welcome to our Church. Maria told me about you. I hope to see you more often," the priest said in a friendly tone.

On the way back to Kiki's house, Maria told her about Peggy. "Peggy might come and visit with you at Kiki's this week," Maria said.

* * *

One afternoon that week, Peggy showed up at Kiki's house. It was Wednesday—Kiki's day off—and Kiki, Silver, and the girls were having dinner at the round table in the kitchen.

"I've come to meet Silver," Peggy said after introducing herself. Peggy was about Silver's age, tall with short, light brown hair and electric blue eyes. She wore her Navy uniform.

"I'm Kiki and this is Silver."

"Does she need a place to stay after you move? That's what Maria told me." Peggy spoke to Kiki, ignoring Silver.

"Yes."

"I have only one question. Is she straight?" "Of course," Kiki said.

What kind of question was that? Maybe, Silver thought, I don't know enough English after all.

"I'm single and own a big house in Mandarin. I'll take her in."

It seemed everything had been arranged for her, without Silver even being consulted.

One afternoon, while the movers packed Kiki's furniture, Maria and Peggy came over and took Silver and her luggage to Peggy's house. Peggy had a nice place, located on the South side of Jacksonville, in an area called Mandarin, about half an hour by car or bus from downtown. The house had three bedrooms and two full bathrooms. She usually rented one bedroom out to friends who were nurses working for the Navy to help with expenses.

Silver moved into one of the two small spare bedrooms, the one at the opposite end of the house from Peggy's bedroom, and the closest to the second bathroom.

The large kitchen and breakfast area, the living and dining room area, and the front entrance were in the middle of the house. It was the ideal arrangement for Silver.

Peggy worked at the Naval Station at Mayport. She left early in the morning and returned after 5:00 p.m. She also took classes at the university. Peggy was very busy and let Silver know right from the beginning that she had to arrange her own transportation.

Jacksonville is a large city. It encompasses 840 square miles, an area as large as New York City and its suburbs. Of course, the population is much less than New York. Jacksonville had about 600,000 residents at that time. The bus system was designed to carry people from one end of Jacksonville to downtown. If you needed to change buses and go in a different direction, you had to first go downtown on one bus to the terminal, change buses, and go in another direction.

To go anywhere by bus was a two-hour trip at least. The buses came every half-hour or so. Most residents had their own cars.

Silver didn't have a car in the beginning, nor a driver's license for that matter. Peggy showed her how to get to the nearest bus station, gave her a spare key to the house, and wished her luck.

Silver learned the bus schedule. She packed a sandwich for lunch and took a bus downtown every day. She usually came back by bus after 5:00 p.m. There were so many things she had to do downtown. She went to English classes, then to the Florida Junior College and stayed there to wait until Mr. Joca, the counselor, had a little time to work with her on her resume.

She first wrote down everything she knew about her education and her experience, describing the kind of engineering jobs she'd done while in Romania and Greece. Then Mr. Joca discussed her writing with her and finally he put her resume together in acceptable English. The secretary at the Junior College typed it for her, and the lady at Social Services made copies.

She had lunch with Mr. Joca and Silviu sometimes. Other times she ate her sandwich at the Main Street library as she searched for technical books.

Silviu, the other Romanian refugee in Jacksonville at that time, was not so lucky. Silviu and Silver were the only ones in Jacksonville. Later on, as the years passed, a lot of other Romanian refugees made Jacksonville their home.

Silviu didn't have Silver's education or brains, and he also had bad luck. He came to Jacksonville by bus from New York City, where he first arrived as a refugee and where he'd stayed for about six months. There, other Romanians took him from the airport and got him to work for them for nothing. Then, he was mugged.

When he arrived in Jacksonville, he didn't know how to speak English and was in a complete state of shock. Social Services contacted Mr. Joca and Rodica, and Mr. Joca took him to this house for about ten days. Silviu was afraid to see or speak to anyone.

Mr. Joca and his wife, who had six children, were kind to him, enrolled him in English classes, and found him a job at the Junior College downtown as a janitor.

Silviu dreamed of becoming an oil businessman, something he saw on the serial "Dallas," which he'd seen in Romania.

When he defected from Romania to Yugoslavia, Silviu risked being shot at the border. He swam across the Danube River at night, risking discovery and getting killed by the border patrol.

"Tell me exactly, how do you think you're going to become an oil businessman? Do you have a plan? Have you figured out how you're going to go from where you are today to where you want to be tomorrow?" Silver asked him several times.

"I don't know, but that's what I want to be. An oil businessman. That's why I came here," Silviu answered.

That didn't seem reasonable to Silver, but she did not tell Silviu so. If that was his dream, who was she to shatter it? Silviu was a young man, rather heavy and short, with thinning brown hair and bad teeth. Maybe his dream was all he had to keep him going.

CHAPTER 6

The Job

When they called from the state office, Silver was in the English class for foreign born people with other refugees at the downtown Main Library.

The clerk interrupted the class. "Is there anybody here by the name of Silver?"

"Yes. That's me." In a fraction of a second, a thousand questions crossed Silver's mind. What can it be? A tragedy. Maybe somebody from the family, back in Romania. Why else would someone try to reach her here?

"You have a phone call. You can take it in the hallway." The clerk led Silver outside the classroom to a phone. "Pick up on the blinking line." "Hello. This is Silver." She felt as if her heart was being squeezed by an enormous hand.

"Hello, Silver. This is Mr. Sapp, the personnel director with the Department of Environmental Regulations. I'm calling to offer you the job as a Stormwater Engineer in our Jacksonville office." His voice seemed calm and friendly. "Your salary will start at around $19,000.00 a year, or $1,600 a month. You can start as soon as you pass the physical examination. What do you say? Will you accept the offer?"

"Yes, of course, I accept." Silver tried to sound as cool as possible and refrained from screaming or jumping up and down. "Will you please tell me what I need to do to get my physical examination?"

"Go to the state clinic located downtown on 8th Street."

She was so happy and relieved! From talking to the other refugees and listening to their stories, she realized how hard it had been for others to obtain good jobs and what slim chances of success they really had. People from all walks of life, of all ages, and all religions, from different corners of the planet, all hoped for a better life here in America; all were deeply scarred by life's hardships, but not defeated. All had the courage to leave everything behind, to cut their roots, and risk everything, even their own lives in hope for a better life, for the promise that America held.

They were all determined to do their best, whatever was required of them to survive and succeed. If not for them, at least for their children.

Of all of them, she was so lucky to be blessed! Her diligent work had started to pay off.

For Silver, in the few days spent here, Jacksonville had become her new home.

She'd already made so many new friends. Dazed, Silver returned to class.

"What was it? Good news, bad news?" the young teacher asked. "Good news indeed. I've been offered a job as an engineer with the state office here in Jacksonville," Silver said.

"How much money are you going to make? Did they tell you?" another refugee asked.

"One thousand six hundred a month," Silver answered, having trouble believing it. "Whoa! Do you know you are going to make more money than my husband and I do together? And that's just a start for you," the teacher said.

The others were overwhelmed by her good fortune; all congratulated her.

She had to wait until eleven o'clock that evening to call home to Romania. It was an established ritual that she called home at eleven o'clock. That was dictated by the economy rates of Southern Bell more than anything else. It was six o'clock in the morning in Romania and her call woke up the entire family.

"Mother, it's me, Silver." The sound was clear as if they were next door. "I have good news. I found a job; we've succeeded," she shouted, her enthusiasm finally getting the better of her.

"What? What are you saying? Did you find a job? What kind of job?" Mother was excited too.

"They offered me a job as an engineer at the state office, here in Jacksonville."

"That's wonderful. That's what we all hoped for, and worked so hard for. We are safe now. Thank God for it.

"Silver, this is your father." His dear voice sounded clear. "We are all so proud of you. We are a hundred percent behind you. You know that, don't you? We cannot wait to be with you again. I slipped your picture, the one you sent me, under the desk glass and I am looking and talking to you every day. We wish you luck in your new job. Hope to see you soon."

"Hi, this is Radu. How much money are they giving you?"
"One thousand six hundred a month. That's dollars."

"Whoa. That seems like a lot of money. Make sure you don't spend all of it. Try to save some for darker days."

"Yes I will."

"We hope we will be together soon." Her mother sounded hopeful. "Mady is dancing around the table. We are very happy for you. Please write more often and tell me everything, all the details."

The hope that they would be reunited soon kept all of them going. The success of one of them meant success for all of them. They were a unit, indestructible and inseparable.

* * *

Mr. Sapp explained to Silver how to get to the state health clinic and after she was given her physical from the clinic, Silver started her new job.

Less than two months had passed from the night she arrived in the United States to the day she started her job, November 24, 1981.

The state office was located in a row of small brick buildings off Emerson Street, close to downtown. Her office was a room with walls paneled in honey-colored wood. Unfortunately, she had no windows, but the close proximity of the main entrance, the noises of people moving past her door busy doing their jobs, and the continuous flow of people kept her on her toes.

Her first day at work, her boss, Mr. Watkins, explained the job to her: she would be conducting the state's new program on storm water. The state was in the process of implementing a new program and rules to control nonpolluting source runoff. She would have to attend training sessions in the central office in Tallahassee before the program took effect. There were rules and regulations she had to read and learn, and then apply them when she checked the engineers' plans and gave them permits to build.

She had to pass her driving test and secure her driver's license since she was expected to drive to sites in Jacksonville and in the neighboring counties. So much to learn.

CHAPTER 7

DEP

Silver made a firm promise to herself: if these people showed her that they believed in her by offering her such a job, she had to do her absolute best and prove to them they were right in choosing her and giving her such responsibilities. She had to rise to the task, as hard as it seemed.

First, she had to pass her driving test. She obtained a copy of the Florida driver's manual and began studying.

For now, her boss, Mr. Watkins, drove her from Peggy's house every morning and back at the end of the work day. He was the only one at the office who lived near Peggy and he also had more free time because he was single. If he'd shown anything besides professional interest in Silver, she never considered it. She had no interest in him except her work.

At work, Silver started to make new friends. There was Kathleen, a woman engineer who was the same age as Silver. She was divorced with two small girls to raise by herself. Kathleen was tall with thick, ash blond hair, and she favored wearing pants and blouses at work. She also had just started working at the state office. She was looking for an apartment for herself and for her daughters.

"Are you interested in finding a place of your own? I mean to rent an apartment and move out of Peggy's?"

"Yes, I've been considering it," Silver said. "I think I'd prefer to be by myself."

"I'm looking for an apartment for me and the girls. Would you like to go during lunch time to look at the apartment complexes nearby, and see if we can find something we like?"

"That's a great idea, Kathleen. Thank you for thinking of me." "Listen, when we go, I'll let you drive my car so you can practice for your driver's exam."

"Are you serious? Aren't you afraid of letting me drive?"

"No, back at the farm in Missouri, where I grew up, I taught a lot of people to drive. It's easy. We'll take the less crowded routes."

"I went to driving school back in Romania and I passed the test. I know how to drive. I don't have much driving experience though and, of course, I don't know the streets here in Jacksonville."

"They're easy enough to learn." Kathleen reassured her.

Silver passed the written examination for her license, and had to come back for the driving test. She had to practice her driving.

Finally, Kathleen and Silver found what they were looking for. There was an apartment complex on the south side of town, not far from their office, in an area with many apartment complexes for rent. Not expensive, but not cheap. The one-bedroom apartment Silver looked at was in a townhouse, with the living room and kitchen downstairs and the bedroom and bathroom upstairs.

"I'll paint the place for you before you move in," the young manager promised.

"That would be great," Silver said, gazing at the empty, beige walls. "Maybe, I could even shampoo the carpet. When did you say you wanted to move? By December first?"

"Yes," Silver said as she stared at the worn, brown carpet. "Shampooing the carpet would be very nice."

"If you like, let's go back to the office. You'll have to pay a month's rent in advance. Do you have the money with you?" the manager asked.

"Yes, I do."

"Then you have to go to the tax collector's office and pay the deposit for the electricity so they know to turn it on the first of the month."

"Where is the tax collector's office?"

"It's here in Mandarin next to the Publix. You know you are quite lucky. We do not ask for a six month lease. There are places in town that ask as much as a one-year lease."

"Yes, I heard about that. It helped make up my mind about this place," Silver said.

Kathleen chose a two-bedroom apartment in the same complex near the end of the row of townhouses. The complex had a swimming pool and a laundry building equipped with coin-operated washers and dryers. The manager took care of the maintenance of the buildings. Silver only had to pay the water and electricity bills on top of the rent. Altogether it came to something like $300 a month, which was all she could afford.

She went ahead and paid the deposit for the apartment and went to the tax collector's office and paid for the electricity to be turned on by the first of the month.

Silver had to let Peggy know she'd decided to move into an apartment starting the beginning of December.

That evening, when Peggy got home from her job, Silver was in the kitchen cleaning, and Peggy joined her later and started cooking rice in the pressure cooker for dinner. The understanding was that Peggy did the cooking since she was very good at it, and Silver cleaned the kitchen and washed the dishes.

"Peggy, I decided to move into an apartment of my own stating December first."

"Good for you. Where is the apartment located?"

"It's near my job. Kathleen and I are moving into the same apartment complex located on Old Kings Road."

"You know those aren't the best apartment complexes in town."

"I realize that, but they are close to my work and the rent and utilities are about as much as I can afford now."

"You're all set then."

"I'll start packing my stuff and I'll move out on the first of December." "Good luck. I can give you few pans and pots for the kitchen, and a chair. Do you have a bed?"

"Maria talked to some friends of hers and they are going to lend me a folding bed and some small appliances for the kitchen. That's all I need right now. The place has its own refrigerator."

"How are you going to get to your job?"

"Kathleen promised to drive me to work and back since we're going to live in the same apartment complex."

"It sounds like you thought of everything."

On the first of December Silver moved into her new home.

The manager did better than just painting the apartment. He had new carpet installed and hung new curtains in the windows. Everything looked nice and clean and fresh.

Not to seem ungrateful to her new friends, but she was happy to have her own place and privacy. Though a lot of singles and young couples lived in the townhouses next door and in the apartment complex, Silver didn't socialize. She was too busy getting herself established, and she already had friends.

CHAPTER 8

The Car

Silver began looking for a car. She asked Mr. Joca to go with her to shop for one. The following Saturday morning, Mr. Joca picked her up at her apartment and they drove to every dealership in Jacksonville. At the Toyota place on Philips Highway, Silver spotted the car that stole her heart. It was a brand new, shiny red Toyota Corolla with a black roof and black interior. The dealer had it displayed in the center of the showroom on a spinning platform. She knew this was the car she wanted to drive, and nobody could convince her otherwise. The car cost something like $7,000 which was a lot of money for anybody, not just for somebody who had recently immigrated to the United States with no money in the bank and knowing no one. Somehow, Silver was convinced she'd get the car.

She didn't have credit established in the USA. She had a good job and good income, but as far as credit was concerned, she was a newcomer. But, she didn't want an old car. She thought it was a waste of money in the long run.

It was her father's teaching she never forgot, that the cheapest way in the long run was always to buy the best quality items which would last the longest.

She asked Mr. Joca to go with her to the state credit union to find out about the possibility of financing a new car. The manager, a nice smart-looking lady, told her "that she might get credit if, after six months she continued to hold onto her job and became a permanent employee. For now, it was too soon for a loan."

"I want to buy a car," Silver told Maria over the phone. "I know what car I want, a red Toyota, but I don't know how to finance it. I went to the state credit union and asked about financing, and they turned me down, at least for now. Do you have any good ideas how I might get the car?" "Well, I'd like to help, but you know I'm in the middle of a divorce and all my money is tied up," Maria said. "But I'll look into it and see what can be done. Where did you say you found the car you want?" Silver told her.

"I know Mr. Bush, the owner of the Toyota place. I'll talk to him about giving you a good price. Also, I'm a friend of the director of Barnett Bank in town and I'll talk to him for you. Maybe his bank will be willing to lend you the money."

"Maria, that's so nice. You know you can trust me. I will not take off and disappear."

"I know I can trust you. I'll see what can be done. Maybe they would be satisfied with me guaranteeing your loan," Maria added.

A few days later, Maria came and picked her up at her apartment and they went to see the director of Barnett Bank. They went into his plush office; the older man was polite and asked Silver a few questions about her job and her background and about the circumstances which brought her from Romania into the free world. It was obvious that he knew and respected Maria from the way he talked to her. He had already drafted a contract for the Toyota, which sat on the desk in front of him; Maria had signed as a character witness. Silver signed on the dotted line and she became the proud owner of the new shiny red Toyota.

It was like a miracle. Silver couldn't believe her good fortune.

By that time she'd passed the driving test and so she drove home to her apartment in her shining new car. Full of joy, she felt like jumping up and down. It had been less than three months since she'd arrived in the United States. She was riding high on a wave and not stopping. With her first paycheck, Silver paid the rent and the utilities for the apartment for that month, put $800 toward the down payment on the car, and with the remaining $150 she thought about having a party for her new friends at her new apartment, in her new country. She had to give thanks first to God for her good fortune, and then to all her new friends who helped her dreams come true.

"Would you like to go and look for furniture at a garage sale nearby?" Kathleen asked. "We can go during lunch."

"How did you find out about the garage sale?" Silver asked. "In today's newspaper."

"I guess we can go. I don't really have the money, but I can look." "Money's not a problem at a garage sale. The furniture there isn't new and so it's relatively cheap."

"Then let's go. For sure I need some furniture and the apartment would look better especially since I've decided to throw a Christmas party," Silver said.

The garage sale was in an apartment building next to their office. They looked through the items and Silver decided on a big plushy sofa of brown velvet in nearly new condition, a round oak dining table that needed its legs tightened, and an oak coffee table and a small round side table. All together they cost less than $200. Kathleen put some of the furniture into her trunk and the rest was to be delivered to Silver's apartment.

Silver invited the young priest from the Greek Orthodox Church in Jacksonville, Father Costopulos, to bless her new home, her food, and her friends. She also invited Mr. Joca and his wife; and Maria and her son and daughter; and Peggy and Kathleen and Rodica. Her small apartment was full of joy and laughter and good fellowship that evening. Silver arranged the apartment tastefully and covered the spare furniture with beautiful embroidered tablecloths her mother had sent from Romania. She bought fresh flowers from the market and cooked all the specialties: Romanian and Greek pastries and other dishes from back home.

The priest blessed her house and the food on the table and the people attending the party.

Silver was grateful for her good fortune and safe landing in her new country, for her new friends, for her new house, for her new car, and her new life. Everybody at the party felt touched by her success story and wanted to be part of it.

CHAPTER 9

Wakula Springs

At the office, Silver had to learn Florida's rules and regulations, the administrative code that dictated all development in Florida. Her job was to review plans for new development and approve them in accordance with the new regulations for stormwater-nonpoint pollution sources.

Silver didn't want anyone to know how hard it was for her to comprehend the arid language of the rules and regulations and to apply them to everyday business.

She had a big Romanian-English dictionary, as well as an academic dictionary from back in Romania developed by the Academy of Romania which included all the technical words of her profession. Every time she found a word she couldn't comprehend, she'd look it up. The stormwater rule was a new program about to be implemented in Florida, and the state was taking small steps toward implementing it. The head office in Tallahassee had started some internal training for stormwater engineers based on the experience and research of faculty and research teams from the University of Florida in Gainesville.

Within the first months of starting work, Silver and her boss were sent to a workshop in the Tallahassee office.

One week before the trip to Tallahassee, Silver was asked into the office of the director. "Are you planning on making a presentation on stormwater treatment at the workshop in Tallahassee?"

"I wasn't planning on it," Silver said, taken aback by the suggestion.

"I think you should give a presentation some consideration. I think you have good experience, and it might be helpful to share it with your colleagues from the other offices."

"I'm working with some consulting engineers on their plans for a new development," Silvia replied. "They are using some innovative ideas on stormwater treatment which I think might benefit the attendees."

"How about doing the presentation, then?"

"I'm very self-conscious about my English. I know I have a strong accent."

"That's foolish. We are a nation of immigrants, all of us. Second, you're going to speak in front of professional people—scientists—who are used to hearing foreign accents. Just remember to talk clearly and slowly."

"O.K., I'll do it."

"Talk to Mr. Sapp in case you need something for the presentation." "Thank you."

Silver started to plan. She only had a week to prepare. She noticed from previous workshops she attended that the speakers used slide projectors and visual display material as they talked. What could she prepare in such a short time?

She went to talk to Mr. Sapp. "I'd like to do this presentation at the upcoming workshop in Tallahassee, but I don't quite know how. I'd like to have a slide presentation and talk at the same time, but I don't know how to prepare the slides."

"Well, it's rather too short notice for slides, but I have an idea. Why don't you prepare the presentation, including graphics, on sheets of 8½ x 11 paper, and then we'll copy the sheets of paper onto transparencies and you can use an overhead projector."

"Do we have an overhead projector here?"

"I think we have one. You can also take along a portable screen, even though I'm sure they'll have one in Tallahassee. Other speakers will need one."

"That sounds good. I'll start working on the presentation."

She knew precisely what she wanted to talk about in her presentation, and she started to write her ideas down on sheets of paper like Mr. Sapp suggested. Then, Mr. Sapp bought the transparencies, and they copied the material onto them. When they were ready, one afternoon in the empty conference room, she set up the overhead projector with Mr. Sapp's help and showed her presentation on the wall. It was good. It worked. She was ready.

Silver's boss drove the state car. The night before they put the overhead projector and the portable screen in the trunk. His secretary made reservations for both of them at the Ramada Inn in Tallahassee.

When they arrived at their hotel, Silver was upset to find out that they had adjoining rooms with an interconnecting door. She first made sure that the lock and chain was secure before she even put her luggage down. She was so upset she developed a migraine. Maybe the boss had designs on her after all. But there was no way Silver would accept any advances from him. She decided to behave so that the older man couldn't even open his mouth to say anything out of line. She wouldn't give him a chance. Silver had heard rumors back at the office about his behavior outside the office—she'd heard that he liked very young girls, and he was seen at nude beaches around Florida. It was just gossip, Silver thought, but what if it was true?

A soft knock on the door disturbed Silver's nap. "Silver, it's me, Mr. Watkins. Do you want to go out and eat this evening?"

She considered not going out with the older man, then reconsidered because they shared the same state-owned car and she was hungry. "Thank you for asking me. I think I'd like to go. I'm hungry. I'll meet you in the lobby in half an hour."

They went to a nice restaurant that Mr. Watkins knew from previous trips. The waiter came by their table and asked for their order.

"I don't think I can eat anything. I have a bad headache." Silver excused herself. Her head was pulsing with pain.

"Not even something to drink?" her boss asked. "Maybe a Pepsi, please," Silver told the waiter.

While her boss enjoyed his dinner and his drink, she sat there miserable, nursing her headache. She couldn't help noticing that at the time they were ready to leave, her boss left a small tip and returned afterwards and took some change back. Silver thought the old man was just cheap.

He was so badly intimidated by Silver and her icy behavior that he never said as much as a word out of line or remotely unprofessional. Ultimately, it was Silver who felt pity for him, but that first night, when she arrived back to the hotel, she was violently sick.

The second day they drove to the Wakulla Springs resort, on the Gulf just outside Tallahassee, where they'd attend the three-day workshop.

It was a beautiful resort, built like a castle among pine trees. They stayed in an old inn, beautifully restored and decorated, located on the edge of the Okefenokee swamp on a clear, spring-fed lake. It was an old, picturesque building with dining rooms downstairs, and a great fireplace in the living room/reception area. Curved wooden stairs led to the upstairs bedrooms; stained glass windows overlooked the spring. The sun filtered through the tall windows in the dining rooms, which were temporarily converted into classroom space for the workshop. Silver could see tourists taking rides in glass-bottom boats on the lake.

The workshop had drawn a mixed crowd of young engineers and environmental specialists, professors from the university, and researchers, all discussing the new stormwater rules and regulations, which were ready to be implemented.

Silver's presentation was scheduled on the first day during the afternoon session. She didn't need the overhead projector or the portable screen they'd brought along, because the resort had a big screen and an overhead projector installed in the classroom. She had carefully prepared her speech to go with the slides the night before they left for Tallahassee. She thought she would be intimidated, but when she got in front of her audience and started talking about technical issues, she forgot where she was and concentrated on transmitting, as clearly as she could, the technical information to her colleagues. The audience asked a number of questions at the end of her presentation, which Silver answered before they moved on to the next speaker.

She was done with it and now she could enjoy the trip like everybody else.

Silver felt at home among the other specialists and was enthusiastic about the open discussions, especially because she was among professional colleagues and was consulted during discussions.

After the classes and presentations that night, they all went to a restaurant as a group and had a lot of fun getting to know each other. Silver almost forgot about her boss. She could pick and choose whom she wanted to drive with since almost everybody in attendance had a car. The next day was Saturday, and they decided that instead of going back to Jacksonville that Friday evening, they would stay one more day and visit the swamp.

They paid for the hotel room for that night out of their own pockets. The next day, they met with a group of environmental specialists who knew the swamp. They all road in two big four-wheeler trucks into the nature preserve. For the first time Silver saw alligators, snakes, including water moccasins, and the marshes, with their wild turkey and deer, all of which are among Florida's most valuable natural resources. Early in the morning the swamp was enveloped in a thick fog, a mist rising from the marshes. They were driving in the four-wheelers on a narrow levee raised above the swamp and on both sides of the vehicle

Silver could see alligators raising their heads and opening their mouths and swarming about in muddy waters.

The following Monday morning at the office, the director met her in the hallway. "Congratulations, I got a good report on your presentation at the workshop."

＊ ✦ ＊

CHAPTER 10

The Classes

Silver learned from Kathleen that engineers had to pass a two-day state examination to become licensed and registered with the state of Florida. Without the test, one could not go far in the engineering profession.

"Have you tried to take it?" Silver asked. They were in Kathleen's office at break time.

"Not yet. I'm studying. I don't want to take the exam unless I'm very well prepared. You can't take it more than five times," Kathleen answered.

"That makes it difficult."

"It's a hard exam. I know a lot of people who took it several times and failed. Phil—here in our office—he tried it seven times and failed. That was before they changed the rules and limited the test to five tries. Finally he gave up and bought an orange grove in South Florida to keep him busy."

"Do you have the books to study from?"

"I have some books. I'll show you what I have." Kathleen took several thick books from the shelves and showed them to Silver.

One day, Silver had to go for a meeting downtown at city hall.

There, she met some older engineers who listened to her story. "Would you like to join the Florida Engineering Society?" an older gentleman, George, who reminded her of her father, asked in a polite tone of voice.

"Could I? I'm not a registered engineer," Silver said.

"You were registered in Romania, weren't you? We'd be proud to have you as a member of the Engineering Society, the Jacksonville Chapter. I'd like to sponsor you if that's O.K. I'll mail you the application and when you've filled it out, send it back to me."

Silver filled out the application, paid the fee, and was admitted as an Associate Member of the Florida Engineering Society. There, she learned about the refresher courses the Florida Engineering Society offered to prepare candidates for the professional examination.

The classes began evenings in January of 1982 at the junior college downtown.

Both Maria and Peggy, and even Silviu, who had been stabbed once while walking downtown at night, warned Silver about the imminent danger of being mugged if she got lost downtown.

Silver got her driver's license and started driving her brand-new Toyota to work every day. She was still unsure of herself and had a hard time learning her way around Jacksonville.

Jacksonville is a sprawling city. Downtown is crowded with narrow one-way streets. Before the first night of class, Silver went to visit Mr. Joca at the junior college and memorized her way around during daylight. She even made herself notes and a map with the street names, and where she had to turn right and left.

Everything looked fairly simple during the day, but that night at 11:00 p.m., after class, she got lost on her way back to her apartment. The streets looked different in lamplight. Silver noted that nobody was walking the streets. Finally, she spotted a gas station and pulled over to ask for directions. Even at the gas station everything was locked up at that time of the night, and the clerk was encapsulated in a bulletproof booth with a small window opening to receive payments.

It was the scariest night of her life.

The clerk cracked the door of the booth carefully. "What do you want?" he asked in a not very polite tone of voice.

"I'm lost. I'm trying to get to the south side of town, on Old Kings Road. Would you please show me on the map where I am and where I should go? I'm disoriented."

"Let me look at your map. We're here at the corner of Laura and State Street. You have to go back on Main Street going south and across the Main Street Bridge. Then take the I-95 South to the University Boulevard exit. Old Kings Road is off Powers Avenue and University Boulevard."

Silver tried to conquer her fear and use logic to find her way in the dark and empty streets. She carefully arranged the street map on the dashboard turned on the reading light and proceeded to drive with caution, following the map and the instructions received from the gas station attendant.

She found her way back to the Main Street bridge, the blue bridge, and from there she recognized where she was and found her way home easily. Safe, behind the closed door of her apartment, could release the tension and fear; she calmed down and convinced herself that the experience was not so bad; after all, she had conquered her fear and arrived home safely.

The refresher classes were in two series of three months, each corresponding to the two days of the state examination: one for the fundamentals of engineering and the second for the principles and practice of engineering.

The classes that had started in January that year were for the second part of the examination, the principles and practice of engineering.

The examinations, as she found out, were given two times a year, in April and in October, at different locations in Florida. You had to have your application with all your degrees and credentials checked and approved by the Board of Professional Engineers before you were admitted to take the examination.

Silver filled out the application, paid the examination fee for both days of the exam, and put together the translation of her engineering diploma from Bucharest and a copy of the translation of all courses and grades she took during the five years she went to the Faculty of Hydrotechnical Engineering in Bucharest. Her diploma, as she found out, was the equivalent of a Master's Degree in Civil Engineering in United States.

Silver applied for the October examination and was approved by the Board of Professional Regulations.

From that moment on she spent the majority of her free time and almost all weekends closeted in her apartment studying for the exams. She was studying familiar concepts, which she had learned some time ago in college, but the concepts were in English and the measurements in English units, different from the metric system used in Europe.

Overall, the challenge was not impossible, but it wasn't easy, either.

CHAPTER 11

The Exam

Silver had no idle time to spend with her friends; they understood how important it was for her to pass the examination.

The examination, especially the first part—the Fundamentals of Engineering—consisted of one hundred forty problems to be solved during the morning session, 8:00 a.m. to 12:00 p.m., and another seventy problems in the afternoon session from 1:00 p.m. to 4:00 p.m. Silver thought she would take up all the available time just to read and comprehend the one hundred forty problems. She really had to know her stuff to be able to respond correctly in such a limited time frame. She'd prepared by solving around five hundred problems before the exam. The English language and the English units were working against her. She had to overcome that obstacle and make up for the extra time it took to read the questions by knowing better than the average American candidate how to solve the problems correctly. Fortunately, a major part of the exam dealt with mathematics, an international language.

Finally she received the notification from the Board of Professional Engineers that she had been approved to take both parts of the examination in October that year, 1982. The examination was to take place in Tampa.

The location was a problem. Silver had never driven outside Jacksonville, and Tampa was on the West Coast of Florida, on the Gulf, about a four-hour drive. She had no idea how to get there, nor how to find the place where the exam was given, or a nearby hotel to sleep the night beforehand.

Those problems scared her more than the examination itself.

Silver knew from working with different engineers in town that there were other engineers in Jacksonville who were going to the exam in Tampa.

"Are you going to take the exam this fall?" she asked an engineer who was working with her from a consulting company in town.

"Yes, I am. Are you?"

"I received the approval from the Board for both parts."

"Are you going to try for both parts at once?" the young man who sat across the desk asked incredulously.

"Yes. What's wrong with that? I prefer to be done and over with it at once," Silver answered confidently.

"It'll be very difficult. Everybody I talk to who tried to take both parts at once told me not to even think about it. It's impossible. Life draining."

"Oh, I don't know. How can it be so hard? I have another problem, though. I don't know how to get to Tampa. Are you going there?"

"Yes. I think they arrange you by alphabetical order and my last name is Crawford, same letter 'C' as yours. But I'll only stay for the first exam and come back the next day."

"That sounds logical."

"Listen, I'm leaving the night before. My wife and I are driving to Tampa after work around 5:00 p.m., the Thursday before the exam. We'll get there by 9-9:30 p.m., maybe 10:00p.m. We'll stay at the Holiday Inn near the convention center where the exam will take place. I have an idea. If you want, you can follow my car and drive behind us all the way."

"That sounds great. Just what I need. Because I'll stay for the full two days, I have to take my own car."

They left Thursday night after work and Silver followed the other engineer's car all the way to Tampa. She remembered it getting dark outside and the heavy traffic in the Orlando area. Her eyes burned from fatigue, but she never lost sight of the car in front of her. When they arrived at the hotel around 11:00 that night, she was exhausted. The next day she had to wake by 6:00 a.m. to be at the examination center by 7:30, but the hardest part of the exam was over.

It was the most difficult exam she had to take in her whole life.

The first day, after the lunch break, at 2:00 p.m., she remembered going to the bathroom and staring in the mirror at herself. Her eyes were red from concentration. She felt like her head was a computer running on overdrive. No time to open any books, or even think. Just read the question and mark the correct answer. Most calculations were done in her head without even using scratch paper. No time for that.

In that bathroom, peering at herself, she had to honestly ask: "Just why am I doing this? I do not need it for my job. I do have a good job and I don't need to take this exam to keep it. I will not be able to do this for two days in a row." She realized that she better calm herself down and do her best, because she would not be happy with herself until she passed this exam—even if it was going to kill her. Coming back another time would be even more difficult.

For Silver, it was unthinkable to take the easy way out, to be satisfied with less when she could reach for more, or to back away from a difficult challenge. She wanted to reach for the stars and catch them.

She returned to the examination room and finished her problems. The next day, she awakened and began the second day with a firm determination to pass.

The drive back to Jacksonville, after the examination, was much easier.

She started out by following another colleague's car, but soon lost it and simply read the signs on the interstate. It took her right home without an incident.

She'd conquered her fears and come out a winner.

CHAPTER 12

Traveling

Silver enjoyed her job at the state office. She learned the rules and regulations, the Florida codes, and she became familiar with the engineering community in Jacksonville. Jacksonville was a relatively small city and everybody in the engineering community knew each other. They met at professional luncheons and dinners and at workshops and seminars. They formed a community of professionals trying to keep up with new developments in the industry, to be the best at what they were doing, and to serve their town and the community, as best they could. They all shared a common trade: everybody was proud of their profession. Silver was accepted as a part of it.

One thing Silver learned about Americans was that they respected hard work; they recognized when one was doing his or her best and respected people for what they were and what they became.

The engineering community in Jacksonville took notice and treated Silver with the respect she deserved by her hard work and integrity.

At the office, Kathleen talked about getting married.

"I met this nice man at my church. I think I'm going to get married," Kathleen said.

"That's great news. The best of all. Congratulations," Silver said, really happy for her friend.

"I don't know. Mother's against it." "Why?"

"Because he's a lot older than me, he's been married before. He has a grown son."

"You were married before, weren't you? You have two children from your previous marriage. I don't see what the problem is."

"My mother thinks it is a real problem. I'd like to have her blessings.

It matters a lot to me."

"Let me ask you a question. Do you love him?" "Yes, I do."

"If that's the case, don't let anybody interfere and dictate what's good for you."

"He loves me very much and he adores the girls. He treats them like they're angels. That's very important to me."

"He sounds like a good man."

"We'll be looking for a house. He doesn't like me living in the apartment with the girls."

"That's good. I'll sure miss having you at the apartment, especially when I locked myself out and needed a place to stay until the maintenance man opened my door," Silver said.

Her life was changing again, for better or for worse.

* * *

That fall of 1982, Maria and Peggy, Silver's friends, planned to go on vacation to Washington D.C. and New York City. Silver decided to go with them. She couldn't contain the excitement of finally visiting New York and Washington, places she'd read about and dreamed about visiting one day.

Peggy, the most traveled of them all, planned the itinerary, and Maria, who had her own travel agency, made the reservations at the hotel in New York City and provided the air plane tickets and tickets for several Broadway shows.

They stayed at the Sheraton on Times Square in Manhattan so they could travel easily to all the attractions.

New York reminded Silver of Europe. It was so different from Jacksonville—she missed seeing people walking in the streets. She missed the feeling that you belong, that you are part of the human race, not an individual closed in a machine speeding on wide empty streets, the intimate connection with other people walking next to the other, brushing one against other.

In New York, they ate at the famous Tavern on the Green, walked around Central Park, went shopping at Sacks 5th Avenue, and attended several shows on Broadway.

Peggy, who belonged to the U.S. Navy, took them to the Navy Reserve and they got free passes for a tour. The guided tour took them by bus to all the tourist attractions in New York: to China-town where they visited a Buddhist Worship Temple and bought souvenirs, to the Statue of Liberty and Ellis Island by boat, to St. John's Cathedral. What a fascinating city with its skyscrapers, alive around the clock.

Saturday afternoon they visited Silver's uncle in Manhasset. They took the subway from Penn Station and traveled for about two hours to a small community on Long Island. Her uncle, her mother's second cousin, prepared a feast for them at his house. Silver and her uncle talked about family history and relatives.

The next morning, Peggy and Maria decided they wanted to attend church services. Silver wanted to visit the Metropolitan Museum of Art and decided to walk there herself. The streets were arranged in a grid and one could find one's way easily. Maria told her that it was dangerous to walk by yourself in New York, but Silver went anyway. What a pleasure to walk the streets. In Central Park, she saw the mimes playing on the sidewalk and the street artists displaying their art.

From New York, they took the train from Penn Station to Washington D.C. The train again reminded Silver of her native country, Romania. Even Penn Station reminded her of the Northern Station in Bucharest, with busy people rushing in all directions.

In Washington, they visited the Florida House, where tourists from Florida could get guidance and help and asked about sleeping arrangements since all the hotels were booked. The staff made arrangements for them to spend the night at a bed-and-breakfast near the center of town.

They visited the Smithsonian Museum and all the monuments and tourist attractions in Washington.

* * *

One afternoon, when they were visiting the Capitol Building in Washington, Maria suggested, "Why don't you go and see if you can get an appointment with our local Congressman from

Florida, the Congressman for District 4 that represents the Jacksonville area?"

"Why?" Silver asked.

"To ask his help to bring your family over from Romania."

"Would he do that for me?"

"Yes. That's what elected representatives do; they help their constituents solve problems they cannot solve themselves."

"Really? I've tried to get help everywhere so that my family can come over. I've gone to the Labor Department in Jacksonville, to the Greek Orthodox Church, to Lutheran Social Services. The answer was the same everywhere: wait until you're an American Citizen in five years after your arrival, and then apply for them to be reunited with you."

"Try and see the Congressman while you're here. You're lucky; Congress is in session now. He's the only one who can help with immigration," Maria insisted.

"Do you think he'll receive me without a previous appointment?" "You have to try. We'll explain we're visiting Washington and we're going to leave the day after tomorrow."

Silver knew that back home her family was selling all their household objects and preparing to come over to America, but had had no luck so far in getting a visa.

They went to the Congressional office building and asked for an interview. They were given one for that same day.

Silver went inside the great chamber, that she assumed was the Congressman's office, and pleaded her case to the Congressman, expressing her apprehension of not being reunited with her family. The Congressman listened to her story and promised to help her. That by itself made the trip worthwhile.

When they came back to Jacksonville, she got a telephone call from the local office of Congressman Chappell, and she began the complicated process of bringing her family over from Romania.

In January of 1983, the notification came from the Board of Professional Engineers that she passed her second day of the examination, the principle and practice of engineering, and that she could retake the first part, which she'd failed, in April the following year.

Silver did and she passed on her second try.

Now she was a professional engineer in the state of Florida and she started to investigate how to advance her career. She first tried at the state office, but in the Jacksonville office all of positions for professional engineers were filled.

She either had to move to another office in a different town, or move to a private company.

She chose the latter.

BOOK II

REA-SILVIA COSTIN, P.E. LOVE STORY

The Intruder

I pressed my face to the wrought-iron gate
even before I bought my entrance ticket
to the amusement park.
Avidly, I searched the crowd for him. . . .
Finally, I spotted him, like an overgrown boy,
dressed in his blue trunk suit,
a huge orange tube in hand,
climbing the steps to the highest flume
and sliding down the water
among the children
splashing into the pool
at the toe of the slide.
Grinning, eyes closed, limbs sprawled,
then seizing the tube again
and climbing the stairs
waiting for the next marvelous experience.

Happily, I shouted out his name.
He turned, looked with myopic eyes toward me.
Suddenly, I realized I had spoiled his fun;
I was the intruder.

CHAPTER 13

Matthew

It began a year ago, in 1982, while Silver was working for the state government. She was in charge of reviewing plans, inspecting and giving stormwater permits for new developments.

Her job was divided between field inspections, office work with various consulting firms, reviewing plans, and issuing permits.

She'd met a lot of men working in the same field.

One day, she was at a site inspecting a new development. She was in the state car gathering her notes and her mark-up plans and getting ready to leave for the office.

Since it was hot outside, she had her car windows down. She was dressed for the field in blue jeans, tennis shoes, and a pink blouse, her hair pulled back in a ponytail.

Wearing Levi's and cowboy boots, his white shirt opened at the neck, a tall young man approached her car.

He crouched and peered through the window, studying Silver as if he owned her. A wide grin spread over his face. He didn't introduce himself; he probably assumed everyone knew who he was. Silver felt herself blush.

She stared back. His soft, golden beard set off his straight white teeth. She noticed that his eyes were blue. Silver had never seen such huge eyes, set wide apart and framed by long golden lashes. His shoulders were broad, and he had short, soft golden hair.

Somehow the word "beautiful" applied to him.

The phrase "Pagan Viking God" came to mind, and he had the arrogance to go with it!

She felt strong magnetic currents emanating from him. It was as though she was naked, body and soul, bared for his view. She felt danger, but was totally powerless, her mind, her strong will, all annihilated by his gaze.

Silver reacted, the only way she knew how to, by being ugly. "What are you staring at?" she asked, frowning.

"At you, of course," he answered unaffected. "By the way, I'm Matthew."

"I'm Silver, and I work for the state office. I'm in charge of the storm water permits."

"I know who you are and why you're here. I designed this job. Do you see anything wrong with it?"

"I have to inspect the sites to make sure that the plans I approved have been constructed accordingly and in compliance with the state rules."

"I know that, and I won't interfere with your inspection. If there's anything I can help you with, I'm at your service," he answered with a superior air.

At his open smile and friendly approach she reacted with a cool manner. She could see the hurt and astonishment wash over his face.

After that first meeting, Matthew stopped to visit Silver every time he had business at the state office. Not that he came specially to see her; his visits were more like an afterthought, after he finished his business. Usually, they discussed projects and technical stuff and rules and regulations pertaining to projects.

Occasionally, they met on job sites or attended workshops and seminars together.

Silver knew Matthew had a girlfriend and continued to act reserved.

Every time Matthew stopped to see Silver, he complimented her on her looks, her dress, and her hair. He made her feel beautiful and desirable.

Silver worked with men regularly, but the relationships were all professional. She dressed conservatively at the office and treated men in a friendly and courteous manner.

After she passed her professional examination and secured her state license as a Professional Engineer, Matthew persuaded her to move to the engineering firm he worked for. Secretly, Silver was pondering the idea of leaving her job with the state to join a private firm, where she could get a position as a professional engineer and grow in her career. She had mixed feelings about leaving the state job, though. Silver remembered what Kathleen had told her: "that the state job was the best job she ever had."

She also felt like she betrayed her colleagues and the director who was so kind to employ her and trust her with the job. She went to the director's office to explain her decision. "I wanted to thank you so much for the opportunity you gave me to work and learn and grow here. You've been like a family for me."

"We know that and we're very proud of you. You're moving on to a better job and more opportunity to grow and learn and get a better salary."

"I'm not very proud of myself. I feel like I've betrayed you."

"That's nonsense. That's what America is all about. Opportunity. Grab them when they cross your path. We wish you the best. Come and visit us when you can."

When she left, one of the secretaries told her, "You know, he will get you one way or the other. No mistake about it. Watch out." She was referring to Matthew.

His reputation as a lady's man preceded him.

CHAPTER 14

Ponce de Leon

Late one evening after Silver and Matthew had attended a technical seminar in St. Augustine, he invited her to dinner. They were sharing the company car, and, if she declined, a cold dinner awaited her in front of the TV set in her one-bedroom apartment.

Matthew chose the Ponce de Leon Country Club located on U.S. 1 on their way back. A Mediterranean style building complex, the place was an old country club and golf resort. At that time and hour the restaurant was almost deserted.

"Could you seat us in a booth by the window, please?" Mathew addressed the waitress as if asking a personal favor.

"I'll see what I can do." The young, plain girl ushered them to a secluded booth in front of a window. The big room was set with small round tables with starched off-white linen tablecloths, lit candles, and freshly cut flowers in tall vases. Nobody played the grand piano in the corner of the big room.

"What do you recommend this evening?" Matthew asked as if he was sharing a secret with the waitress.

"We have escargot as an entrée, and the steaks are very good. Also, the swordfish is fresh."

"We'll have the escargot to start, and we'll both take the grilled swordfish."

Silver was flattered and impressed with his knowledge of food and didn't even think to order for herself. She'd established him as the expert and basked in his knowledge.

Matthew ordered a fine white wine from the list.

They completed the dinner with coffee and amaretto liqueur.

Silver and Matthew talked and, gazing into each other's eyes, told stories of their lives. The waitress who served them was very attentive and stayed close by, trying to anticipate Matthew's every whim.

"What are you doing after you finish here?" Matthew asked as she hovered nearby.

"I'll go home and have a nice long, hot bath. My girlfriend will be home by then and have dinner ready."

"That sounds good," Matthew said.

After the girl left, he whispered, "She has to be gay." "How did you figure that out?" Silver asked.

"She's looked at you more than me. Didn't you notice?"

"No, and I don't think you're right. She's trying to please you," Silver said.

Matthew had a way about him that amazed Silver. He entered the most exclusive places and most elegant restaurants as if he owned them. Matthew liked and enjoyed good food; watching him eat was almost a sensual experience. He was familiar with the different dishes that restaurants offered and took delight in savoring the food. Silver never paid much attention to food. Matthew taught her the pleasure of eating a good meal.

After dinner they walked outside and drove to the Bridge of Lions in St. Augustine and lingered there, gazing at the moon and the stars reflected on the Matanzas River.

Once back in town, each returned home.

CHAPTER 15

The Greek Festival

Silver worked the "food line," wearing her Romanian outfit, which was a little different from traditional Greek garb. She was full of joy and felt connected to the Greek community. That night, she worked long hours with the women from the church, taking time off from her office work to serve in the food line. The prior winter, she'd taken time from her job to cook the baklava, the <u>pastitzio</u> and the <u>dolmates</u>, the <u>coulouretzi</u> and the <u>saraillies</u> with the other women. The food had been frozen and stored until the festival in September.

The ladies of the Greek Orthodox Church in Jacksonville had worked long and hard since January of that year, 1983, to prepare and then freeze the food for the Greek Festival.

In Jacksonville, the festival took place every year in September. The celebration was a way to keep the tradition of food, dance, and music alive for the Greek community in town, as well as to familiarize the entire community with Greek traditions. It was also a way of raising funds for the church.

The ladies of the church spent their time volunteering long hours cooking and serving at the festival. Some of them were well established, with husbands who provided for them and their families; others were widows living on their Social Security checks. Each one gave freely of her time and talents.

After three full days of the festival, the ball was held on Saturday night. The Greek Orthodox Church rented the huge exhibition hall on the river next to the Center for the Performing Arts.

The hall was decorated in blue and white, the colors of the Greek flag, with two long food lines on each side of the hall, and a raised platform in the back of the hall for the band and dancers. The platform was decorated with white antique columns resembling the Parthenon. In front of the platform was an open, circular space for dancing; round tables and chairs with seating for ten people occupied the remainder of the huge hall.

Americans came and ate their food and left and the Greeks were serving and dancing and singing and counting the money they made. The women of the church were bone-tired and it showed on their faces and in the way they moved. But when the music started, they were the first on the dance floor, holding hands and dancing the traditional dances.

Sometimes a man would lead the row with a handkerchief in his hand, jumping and rotating, and a row of women would follow, swinging gracefully to the music's rhythm.

Some of the Greek women wore traditional costumes: the full, long, white pleated skirts and white bouffant blouses with blue embroidered vests on top.

The youth of the church dressed in traditional costumes and danced for the audience.

But the real Greek dancers, the men, would dance in pairs. The audience would form a circle around the dance floor clapping hands to the music's rhythm, and two of the best dancers, men, would start dancing by facing each other with a half glass of wine balanced on their forehead.

It was a show worthy of the audience's applause as the men competed in skill and endurance.

Silver watched the people and the dancers with awe. She wanted to feel that she belonged somewhere. It had been almost four years since she'd left her native Romania. All her family was still there.

She was alone now in the Unites States; the closest environment to her native country was the Greek community. Her mother was from Greece, and Silver grew up listening to stories about Greece and the dances and customs as if it were a far away, dream-like country.

She'd spent a year in Greece before coming to the United States. She thought she knew Athens better than her native city, Bucharest. She knew a little bit of the Greek language and felt closer to the Greek community than any other community in America.

It took a long time for the people of the Greek church and the ladies of the church to accept her. After all, she was not a hundred-percent Greek. Her father was Romanian, and she had grown up in Romania. She came to the United States as a refugee without money.

Silver had heard back in Greece that the only God the Americans knelt to was the almighty Dollar.

People judged you by how much money you had. They did not look at who you were, or care about your feelings and sensitivities, or your education and culture.

Silver came with no money at all. The only treasures she had were a good education, a quick mind, and above average looks—and she was young and healthy.

Silver did have an unsinkable belief that all the good things in life were there for her. She knew deep inside that if she worked hard, doors would open for her. Of that, she was certain. Breaks had started to go her way, as she knew they would.

Silver did not ask for charity or a handout or anything that couldn't be obtained without hard work.

People had told her in past that she was naive. Maybe so. She never gave a serious thought to their comments. It hurt her to think people could be bad and mean or have vile intentions. How could that be, when deep within her soul she knew there was God and goodness in everybody? She believed that if you treated people right, they would respond in kind. If mean people had hurt her in the past, she would just turn away from them with no bitterness. Each time she believed more firmly that only good would happen to her.

She simply blocked out of her mind and heart the ugliness and the brutality, and of course, sometimes the inevitable truth.

CHAPTER 16

The Ball

Saturday night, the evening of the Greek ball, Silver wore a long, sleeveless turquoise gown made of the sheerest and softest Romanian cotton embroidered with tiny peach flowers. The green of the gown complemented her hazel eyes. A bit of green eye shadow accentuated the deepness of her eyes. The sleeveless gown revealed her bare arms and shoulders.

Her sensitive eyes and mouth, her pearly complexion, and a svelte athletic body were Silver's best features.

That evening, Silver reserved a table near the dance floor for her guests. She'd invited her good friend Gwen, Matthew, and his girlfriend to the festival.

Silver had met Gwen a few months before at church. Gwen was of Greek heritage and had just moved to town from Ohio. She was single like Silver, and they shared a lot of Greek family values and traditions. Gwen was short and very fashionably dressed in designer clothes.

Her thick, dark brown hair was highlighted and perfectly groomed.

Matthew was tall with blond hair and blue eyes and bearded. He was dressed casually in blue jeans and a white shirt, open at the neck. Matthew brought his girlfriend, Pam, who was also very tall and slender, dressed in comfortable slacks and a blouse.

It was Matthew who had convinced Silver earlier that year to quit her government job and start working with an engineering firm in the private sector.

They'd just started working together, yet Silver already had a great respect for Matthew. He was bright and hardworking, different from many of the other American men she met.

At the table, Matthew ordered Greek sweet wine "Mavrodafi," on Silver's recommendation, and they all tasted the Greek food.

When the music started, Silver danced with the ladies from the church. She was conscious of Matthew's eyes following her closely. Her usually pale complexion was heightened by the wine and dancing. She knew she was enticing Matthew, swinging her body graciously in rhythm. She was usually self-conscious and reserved at work, and she dressed conservatively. The wine, the music, the dances that she loved— all the excitement of the ball relaxed her carefully guarded demeanor.

It was the first time Matthew could see beneath her carefully controlled façade, the first time he could see her dressed in something romantic and revealing, and he couldn't take his eyes away from her. His girlfriend Pam had to sense the undercurrents, but seemed to ignore them for now. She talked to Gwen and, enjoying the Greek food, chose to look the other way, for now.

The attraction of that year's Greek festival was a young, handsomely dark Greek singer.

The band sang Greek songs; the light was dim in the big room and the Greek performer started to sing. He was a willowy young Greek, dancing and singing on top of the tables. The women screamed for his attention and invited him to dance on their tables.

Eventually, the Greek singer came to Silver's table and started dancing on top of it. His soulful singing and his handsome good looks opened a closed door in Silver's heart. It reminded her all too well of Greece and Athens, the places she has been to and maybe never would see again.

At the end of the song, the Greek singer bent down and kissed Silver fully and passionately on the mouth. It was something unexpected for Silver and acted as a catalyst on her already heightened spirits. She felt the pull of love in the air.

Immediately after that, they all left. It was close to midnight and Silver wanted to get to her car and drive home.

She was a little tipsy from the wine and the excitement, but she thought she could handle it.

Outside, the night was warm and pleasant. Gwen and Pam walked a bit ahead, talking.

Silver and Matthew followed behind them. Matthew pleaded for a kiss, the way she'd kissed the Greek dancer at the table. Silver was reluctant. As lightheaded as she was, she knew the danger of impromptu romance. In the back of her mind she knew that she's be opening Pandora's box.

Silver was not a short girl, but Matthew towered over her. He took her in his arms and kissed her deeply. Silver had been kissed before; she had been in love before, but this time she lost control. It was as if a dam had broken, and all her pent-up emotions flew freely from her heart. Her body melted against Matthew's.

It was just a kiss.

Matthew and Silver caught up with Pam and Gwen and Matthew maneuvered to take Silver and Gwen in his car, while Pam drove separately.

"Look, you're pretty drunk tonight," Matthew said, "You're not going to be able to drive safely to your place tonight."

"I'll be O.K. I'm not that drunk," Silver insisted, suddenly afraid. "No, I'm not going to let you drive! We'll all go by my place, and we'll see from there," Matthew said in a resolute tone of voice.

"Pam, you drive my car back to my place. Gwen, Silver and I will go in Gwen's car. Silver is going to leave her car here overnight. Nothing will happen to it. There's a security guard on duty all night. Tomorrow she'll come and get her car."

He was addressing Pam as if she and he were the only two grownups, Silver thought through the thick fog in her head. She and Gwen were just children who needed to be taken care of, needed someone to make decisions for them.

"That's all right with me," Pam said coolly. "I'll see you at your place in few minutes."

Matthew talked Gwen into driving, and he and Silver sat in the back of the car kissing all the way to Matthew's place. Some rational thought crept back into Silver's brain. She was afraid of the consequences at work as well as with Matthew's girlfriend.

CHAPTER 17

The Jacuzzi Party

On the night of the Greek Festival Ball when they arrived at Matthew's house, Silver realized that showing off her true feelings could prove disastrous for her job situation as well as for herself. It was too late though, she'd already done it.

Matthew lived in a small, spotless house. It had a living room/dining room/kitchen combination in front and four bedrooms on the side. Outside the closed patio, he'd installed a huge Jacuzzi in the open area next to the house toward the backyard. There was a roof over the Jacuzzi; otherwise it was open all around, except for the back wall of the house.

Pam led Silver and Gwen with her back to the bedroom. Pam was living with Matthew at the time. She had been married twice before and had a lot of experience with men.

Matthew wanted the four of them to get into the Jacuzzi. Silver was reluctant.

She didn't feel comfortable about the situation. "I don't have a bathing suit with me," Silver said to excuse herself.

"Don't worry about it. Choose whatever you like." Pam opened the lower drawer of the bedroom chest and showed the two girls a collection of bathing suits.

Silver thought it strange that Pam owned so many as she only owned two. Pam changed into a one-piece suit and waited for Silver and Gwen to change.

Silver chose a small bikini. She knew her body was taut and fit. She worked hard to keep it in shape. She took aerobic classes regularly and lifted weights at the Health Club at Baymeadows Apartments, the posh, "yuppie" place for singles where Gwen lived.

Usually, at work or even social events, Silver was careful to conceal her body. She didn't invite unwanted attention from men. Tonight, because of the excitement at the Greek festival and the wine she'd drunk as well as the kisses she'd shared with Matthew that evening, she felt daring. She wanted to display her perfectly chiseled body for Matthew. "When he sees you like that, he'll take you to bed tonight instead of me," Pam said, and changed her full one-piece into a skimpier one.

They all joined Matthew in the Jacuzzi, and Matthew offered all of them drinks.

They relaxed and visited for a while until the time came for Silver and Gwen to go home. Silver was still in high spirits because she'd had too much to drink.

Pam invited Silver to stay for the night with her and Matthew, adding, "The guest sleeps in the middle." Silver didn't understand what Pam meant.

But she knew she didn't like the way Pam talked or behaved. If Silver had any thoughts of backing off from a relationship with Matthew for Pam's sake, that night she decided that Pam wasn't worthy for her to back off. She simply decided she didn't like Pam. Silver was still high- spirited and noticed that Matthew took Gwen aside and talked to her.

In the car, going back to Gwen's house Silver asked Gwen, "What did he tell you?"

"He talked to me about you. He was concerned about you being tipsy and asked me to drive you to my place to spend the night."

"And what else did he say?" The fog in her head had started to clear. "He knows that you like him. He told me that he thinks that's not a good idea since you work together."

"Probably not," Silver admitted. She knew for a fact that a relationship at work was not good.

"When the two of you were back there in the car in the back seat kissing, it reminded me of myself. Once I was in the same situation. Somebody else was driving and this fellow and I were in the back seat necking. We were very much in love. I understand how you feel," Gwen said.

"Now that I can think clearly, I'm scared. I wish it had never happened."

"What are you going to do?" "I don't know," Silver said.

Matthew had told Silver that he had been married before to a nice, strong Catholic lady, Carole, whom he'd met and fallen in love with in college. The strict Catholic upbringing of his wife clashed with Matthew's ideas of enjoying life to the fullest, including women.

They divorced and Matthew swore he would never remarry. He liked his freedom too much.

Pam was the same. They had an easy, comfortable understanding with no obligation on either party.

CHAPTER 18

The Silver Springs

Silver knew she was in love with Matthew. When she thought back, she knew she'd fallen in love with him from the first moment she set eyes on him. It was not a good idea for her. She loved him too much, and she was not sure about his feelings toward her. Pam was still in his life, and Matthew felt comfortable with her around.

All her life, Silver had searched for love, and all her life love had avoided her. Time and again she entered in a new relationship with all her heart only to end up with nothing. Love, like sand, fell through her fingers. The harder she tried, the less she got out of relationships.

This time she was ready for love and decided to make it work.

Silver remembered learning in college that time had a strange property; it could expand, depending on the speed one traveled. It was exactly how she felt when she was with Matthew. It was as if a window had opened for her and time had expanded.

Even a few hours spent with him seemed like days. She thought that the saying, "your life can pass you by without even noticing it," or that, "one can sleep one's life away," were so true. Passing on life's opportunities to fall in love happened to her before she met Matthew.

She felt like she had just awakened from a long sleep.

Silver and Matthew attended a workshop in Orlando. They cut classes short that day so they'd have more time for themselves on the way back home. They traveled in Matthew's car, an old, blue, Lincoln Continental. It suited Matthew. It was big, the way they used to build cars in America back in 60s and 70s—and very comfortable. It had wide, soft leather seats, not like modern cars with narrow, separate driver's and passenger's seats, but one, long comfortable bench. Silver got close to Matthew, leaning her head on his shoulder as they drove, or massaging his stiff neck and shoulders. They stopped at McDonald's, bought some Big Macs and coffee at the drive through window and kept driving and eating, enjoying each other's company.

On the way back to town they stopped at Silver Springs State Park. The early afternoon was warm and sunny. The park was wooded and had picnic tables and restrooms where Silver changed into her bathing suit. She'd learned to put her bathing suit in her luggage every place she went. In Florida it was inevitable they would find water somewhere nearby, and both she and Matthew liked to swim.

One day, Matthew told her he thought they'd been together in a previous life, probably aboard a ship.

They changed into their bathing suits and went to the spring. There was a small beach on a hill sloping down to the water. They put their towels on the beach and went into the warm, clear water. It stayed at a constant temperature year around. Silver could see the rocks on the bottom of the spring and the caves the water came out of.

Matthew, who was an accomplished swimmer, had goggles he lent to Silver. They swam beneath the water's surface and looked through the clear water to the spring's bottom.

Later, they rented a canoe from a park ranger and launched it into the small creek flowing from the spring through the woods. The creek was narrow at its beginning and very clear. It was only about two feet deep next to the spring. They could see the creek's bottom as the canoe slid soundlessly downstream. Trees and branches loaded with Florida moss hung over the water's surface. The sun filtered through the branches. The only sound was that of the birds. It was as if they were the only two people on earth and time stood still.

Silver thought that what she had heard about being in love and all your senses being heightened was so true. It was as if she saw the beauty of nature for the first time and was amazed by it; like her soul was soaking in nature's marvels like a dry sponge.

CHAPTER 19

Home Alone

Silver thought of her moments spent with Matthew as pearls on a string and she cherished them as such. She didn't ask for more.

Silver had been in her mid-twenties when she'd come to the United States, having just finished college in Bucharest, Romania.

She was brought up in a family with strict morals. The right thing for a girl was to save herself for her husband. In school and then college, she had a lot of studying to do and not much time for romance and dating. Sex before marriage was out of question in the strict environment in which she'd grown up.

Silver met and dated several young men before meeting Matthew, but every time something was missing. Either she didn't love him or he didn't love her. Before Matthew, she had never meet anyone she felt she wanted to be intimate with.

This time, she knew she wanted to be with Matthew. Somehow in the back of her mind she knew that as satisfying as platonic love was for her, she knew it would not be enough for Matthew. She started to think of her virginity as an obstacle in the fulfillment of her love. She discussed her feelings with Matthew. It seemed like she could discuss everything openly with him. Above all, he was her best friend.

Matthew was reluctant to start a sexual relationship with Silver. The way he explained it, he was not ready for commitment; he enjoyed his freedom too much and was not sure he could emotionally handle a relationship with her.

One late evening when Pam was away for the weekend, Matthew invited Silver over for dinner.

He never ceased to amaze Silver with his diverse abilities. He cooked a full dinner by himself and arranged it beautifully on the dining room table. He grilled the steaks to "perrrfection," as he liked to brag, adding all the appropriate herbs and spices. The grill was just outside the kitchen on the patio and he went back and forth between the grill and the oven. He baked small, red potatoes and prepared a Caesar salad. As he deftly worked, Silver watched him while drinking Russian vodka.

Together they set up the dining room table with nice china and candles and fresh flowers. While they ate, Matthew talked about his past loves and relationships, and about Carole, his ex-wife. Silver was spellbound.

"You know, I met my wife in college. Carole was studying to be a mathematician. She was smart and wanted to get a job with NASA. I was this country boy. No way could I match her intelligence. I was at Georgia Tech, in Atlanta, studying to become an engineer and she attended a college in South Florida going for her masters. While she was away, I had a relationship with another girl on campus, but I knew that I wanted to marry her. It was just passing time for me."

"What about this other girl?" Silver asked. "Maybe she thought it was serious, that you loved her and wanted to be with her."

"No. I told her how things were, and she accepted the situation for what it was."

"What happened to your wife?"

"When we both finished school we married."

"But what happened? If you loved her like you said, then why aren't you together now?"

"She wanted children, and that didn't happen."

Silver's heart sunk. She wanted children. Ever since she had been a little girl playing with dolls, her most cherished desire was to have children. "That's O.K. People adopt children if they can't have them."

"Yes, that's what we both decided, to adopt a child. And so we did." "So what happened?"

"I love women. And she was a strong Catholic. She couldn't put up with my fooling around."

"If you loved her, why did you do fool around?" "I don't know. It's in my nature, I suppose." "So, what happened?"

"We divorced and she found herself a nice man. Now she has four children. I hope she's happy."

"What happened with to child that the two of you adopted?" "He's with her now. I signed the adoption papers over to her new husband. It was the most difficult thing I had to do in my entire life, but it was the best for the boy.

He has special needs and it was best for him to be with his mother." "She sounds like a fine lady to me."

"She is and I still love her. I'll always love her, I suppose."

"What's with Pam?"

"Pam understands my nature and doesn't ask for more. My relationship with Pam is one of survival."

"And how are you?"

"I like women. I appreciate them for what they are, another human being. I like to touch as many people's souls as I can."

"And the way to touch their soul is to sleep with them?" "That's one way to do it."

"What about me?"

"You are there in my soul too. And you have the potential to became the most loved of all."

"I want to be the only one. I want it all," Silver said.

"You can't have it. There is my first wife who'll always be there, and a friend of mine, a young man I went to college with, and Pam. She is there too. And of course there's my first love."

"And who was that?"

"A girl I knew before my wife. We lived together for one year. Then she decided she liked women better and left me."

"What?"

"Just what you heard. How could I compete with a woman? When she left, I was totally devastated. I thought of ending my life. I took the catamaran we had and went out on the ocean during a storm. But I know I really wanted to live because when the wind and storm became violent, I struggled to save the boat and myself. Since then, I've become a survivor. I don't put my eggs all in the same basket."

"Exactly what's your relationship with Pam? I don't quite understand it."

"You wouldn't. We have an understanding. We do our own thing. No strings attached. She understands me. My wife used to make me feel guilty. I don't want to ever feel like that again."

Silver felt sad. For all his bragging and macho behavior, Silver could sense the different story, the little boy, scared to be left alone, trying to surround himself with as many people as possible. He was afraid to take the chance of loving just one person. What if that person should leave him? He didn't dare put all his emotions in one basket, as he said. It was the vulnerable side of Matthew's character that ultimately drove Silver to him. She harbored an illusion that perhaps her love could change and erase the sadness and fear from his soul. He was like a bird with a broken wing, and Silver took on the challenge of healing him.

There it was. All out in the open. At least she was getting into it with her eyes wide open. She realized that she probably would be better off running away from Matthew as fast as she could. She should have remembered what her mother had taught her about family values. But she was tired of running away from life.

It really would have been the smart choice to run away. But, then, what is life without love?

After dinner, Silver washed the dishes and put them away and both of them changed into swimsuits and went to the outside jacuzzi.

The stars shone above them as they climbed into the water, kissing and caressing and learning about each other's bodies.

Matthew understood Silver's fear of intimacy, her inhibitions about sex and didn't rush her. As he told Silver, "I'm taking my time to smell the roses."

CHAPTER 20

The Wekiva River

Matthew owned a motor home, a camper, and a small boat that he kept on a rented lot at the Wekiva Fishing Camp, famous for its bass fishing.

One Sunday, early in the morning around 5:00 a.m., Matthew came and picked Silver up from her apartment to go fishing for the day. Silver had never been fishing before. They both wore tee shirts and blue jeans over their bathing suits. On the way to Palatka, they stopped in Baldwin at State Road 301, and brought Egg McMuffins and freshly brewed coffee from McDonald's. They ate while driving. Matthew brought fishing rods, and when they arrived at the fishing camp, they stopped at the local convenience store where Matthew bought worms. He chatted with the store manager about fishing and the best bait. It seemed everyone knew him.

Silver and Matthew attached the boat and its trailer to the car and drove to the boat ramp on the Wekiva River. After they launched, they filled the reservoir with gas, and loaded the cooler with beer and their lunch.

They didn't bring any hats with them and the sun was up, beating hot on their heads. Matthew showed Silver how to set the rod and put the bait on it and how to pull the line. They sat quietly for about an hour, but didn't have any luck.

It was getting hotter, so they decided to head up the river all the way to the Rodman Lake and Dam.

In the 1960s, the Army Corps of Engineers worked for the Florida Barge Canal. They built the locks on the river, and the dam that formed Rodman Lake. Later, the lake became a fisherman's paradise. When the idea of the barge canal was abandoned, there was talk about removing the locks and the dam and restoring the river to its natural environment. But people didn't want to give up the fishing.

They started speeding. They ate and drank the cold beer and got a little drunk. The river was beautiful as it meandered through the woods. Its waters were clear and smooth as a mirror. The huge trees on the river's edge reflected on the water's surface. They passed through a set of locks, waiting their turn as the Coast Guard assisted each boat.

They approached Rodman Lake and they could see the tips of the trees that had been submerged at the time of the dam's construction. They had to drive more carefully through the tree-tops. They arrived at the dam and pulled the boat to one side and anchored it. They went by foot to the other side of the dam.

On their way back home that day they stopped and ate fried fish at the camp's restaurant. Silver had never paid much attention to food before she met Matthew. But now with him sharing food, delighting in it, it made the mundane act almost sensual.

CHAPTER 21

The Accident

Silver never ceased to be amazed by Matthew's boundless energy. Matthew could work virtually all day. Even on four hours sleep, he was still full of energy. Silver, on the other hand, if she didn't have her eight-hour sleep, felt grouchy and sleepy all day. Her constitution was more fragile.

Matthew owned an old motorcycle. He often showed up at Silver's apartment late at night, sometimes after she had already gone to bed, waking her up to take her for a ride on the motorcycle. At that time of the night, the roads were empty, and they drove on Interstate 95 and sped on the motorcycle. Matthew told her, "Just trust me and relax. I know it's hard to do, to put your life in somebody else's hands. But that's how it works on a motorcycle. Put your arms around me and stay close. Follow my every movement with your body while I'm driving."

Silver tried to follow the instructions and relax. The two of them formed a whole and took the sharp bends safely without fear of accidents. Silver enjoyed the rides and the speed, but sometimes thought that it was not easy to trust somebody else with her life.

One night, Matthew was working late and called Silver from work, "I'll finish here within a half hour and then I'll stop by your place. It would be nice to have something to eat. I'm starving. I've been working non-stop at this project that has to be ready by tomorrow. I'll see you in a bit."

He rode his motorcycle to work that day.

Silver prepared dinner and waited for him. The half-hour passed by, but Matthew didn't show up. That was not unusual for him. Silver thought at first that he was caught up in work and forgot the time. She called the office, but nobody answered the phone.

She started worrying and didn't know what to do or whom to call.

She just waited.

Within another half-hour Matthew called her, "Hi! It's me." "Where are you? Why aren't you here? What happened?"

"I had an accident with the motorcycle." "Where are you now? Are you O.K.?"

"I'm fine. I checked myself into the hospital."

Silver started to cry. It was, of course, all her fault. He was hurrying to come and see her. That's why he had the accident.

"I was rushing to come to your place and the front wheel of the motorcycle slipped on a manhole cover near the curb. It tossed me over the motorcycle and onto some grass. That was lucky."

"Did you break anything?"

"I don't know yet. The doctor will see me tomorrow. They took x-rays at the emergency room, but didn't tell me if anything's broken."

"How do you feel? I'll come over to the hospital right now."

"No. You better not. It's late and I'm fine. I'll go to sleep now. They gave me some pills. Come tomorrow morning about eight o'clock, after the doctor sees me."

"How did you get to the hospital?"

"I'm here at the hospital next to the office. I walked over." "I suppose the motorcycle is wrecked."

"I think so. I left it behind."

Ironically, Pam worked at that hospital.

Silver could not wait for the night to pass. First thing in the morning, she went to see Matthew. By that time they put him into a room, and he was sleeping. When he woke, he saw Silver sitting in a chair by his bed.

"Hi! Are you O.K.?" Silver asked, softly. "Now that you're here, I'm fine."

"What did the doctor say?"

"I cracked a vertebra. He'll talk with the orthopedic specialist and let me know. For now, he told me to stay in bed on my back for a few days."

"It sounds terrible. Are you in pain?" "They gave me something for pain."

"I brought you a yellow rose, and a unicorn to cheer you. I always think of you as my unicorn." Silver knew that Matthew was colorblind and the only color he could see was yellow.

"Are you going to stay a while longer?" "Yes, I'll stay here with you for a while."

"Then, I can go back to sleep. I feel really drowsy."

"I'll be sitting here when you wake up, don't worry," Silver said.

Silver stayed with him as he slept. He awakened for a few minutes and talked to her again. She held his hand. Pam hadn't seen him yet. He'd also called her to tell her what had happened and where he was.

Probably the other nurses, who knew Pam, reported on Silver being at his bedside.

Later that afternoon Pam showed up with some flowers and balloons. Silver left and as Matthew told her later, Pam asked him about his relationship with Silver. Matthew confirmed that he loved Silver, but Pam assured him that would not be a problem for her. She said she'd date somebody else, but would wait in the wings in case something happened. Silver began to detest Pam even more. She recognized Pam's game as playing the "nice lady" for what it was.

Silver knew Pam was using her extensive knowledge of men to deal with the situation with Matthew. Silver was convinced that Pam didn't love Matthew. She just didn't want to give him up.

Strangely enough, Matthew appreciated the way Pam handled herself and the situation.

Every day after work, Silver stopped at the hospital to see Matthew and bring him up to date with the office happenings. She would bring his work over and discuss it. She took a novel with her, and read while Matthew slept.

Finally, they released him from the hospital. He was supposed to wear a back brace for a few weeks. To Silver's utter relief, there was no permanent damage to Matthew's spine.

CHAPTER 22

The Busch Gardens

One weekend after Matthew returned to work, he and Silver went to Tampa's Busch Gardens. Since they both enjoyed thrilling rides, Matthew challenged Silver to ride the "Scorpio" with him. They left really early in the morning and arrived in Tampa by mid-morning. First thing, they lined up for "Scorpio."

"Are you up for the big ride?" Matthew teased. "Or are you going to chicken out? You know, I drove all the way here just to ride the 'Scorpio'?"

"I'm going to ride it if it kills me," Silver said. "It's a challenge, I have to do it! Only, I wish I hadn't had that V-8 this morning."

Silver was as excited about the ride as Matthew. They both climbed in the car and the ride started with a steep slope followed by twists and turns. At full speed, the cars turned upside down. Silver kept her eyes closed for most of the ride, and screamed at the top of her lungs along with everybody else.

When the ride ended, Silver felt sick to her stomach, nauseated from the motion. They sat on a bench, first thinking it might be a passing sickness. When Silver started to feel worse, they went to the park's first aid office. The nurse gave Silver some kind of orange-looking, mint- tasting liquid to drink, and she lay down for a few minutes. The liquid didn't help at all. For Matthew's sake, she went with him and tried to enjoy the scenery. They saw the animals and Matthew went on a few rides by himself.

Silver was still sick and Matthew was tender with her. They sat on a bench and he tried to feed her small pieces of bread.

When she felt really sick again, he went with her and held her head while she threw up. Silver thought he was wonderful.

When they finally left, Silver was still sick. Spasms racked her body. She'd ridden rides before and never been sick, nor was she ever sick for such a long period of time.

She thought Pam wishing her dead had somehow something to do with her sudden sickness.

On the way back in the car she pressed against Matthew on the front seat.

"Why don't you lie down?" Matthew said, the concern in his voice apparent to Silver. "Put your seat back and try to sleep."

"I thought about it, but then I'm afraid I'll die and not be with you, not holding your hand. I prefer to stay here crouched with you."

"Then unbuckle your seatbelt and lie down. Put your head in my lap. That way you can sleep and still be near me."

"That sounds good." Silver stretched herself out and nestled her head on Matthew's lap. She felt better already. By the time they reached home, she felt better.

CHAPTER 23

The Confrontation

That Friday morning, Silver and Matthew were supposed to go to a workshop in Tallahassee. As usually, Silver counted on riding with Matthew in his car. The company paid mileage for the employees using their personal cars on business trips. Her own car, the red Toyota, was getting old and the air conditioning was broken. She didn't have the time or the money to fix it right away. Driving without air conditioning in Florida was insufferable. Silver had lived in Florida for almost four years, but her body hadn't yet adjusted to the heat and humidity. That day, she wore her best business suit and took special care about how she looked. She knew she'd probably spend the day with Matthew and was looking forward to it.

When she arrived at the office that morning, she found Matthew busy with papers, drawings, and computations. He'd worked the night before straight through, readying a project. Something went wrong with the survey and he was trying to figure out what.

He could not accompany Silver to Tallahassee that day. She had to go alone and take her own car.

That ruined the mood for the day. She felt frustrated by not being notified in advance so she could fix her car for the trip and about not spending the day with Matthew.

She called Matthew from the hotel in Tallahassee where the seminar was being held. They decided Silver should come back after the seminar that evening to his house. They could at least have dinner together. Silver's mood lightened as she looked forward to the evening.

When the seminar was over, she drove back into town as quickly as she could. After five hot hours in the car and a full day of seminar, she was exhausted and felt the need for a shower. Her new, expensive suit was ruined with perspiration, but her spirits soared at the expectation of being with Matthew.

Matthew told her that Pam had moved out, and was away for the weekend with her boyfriend, and Silver never gave the situation another thought.

Matthew did give her his garage door opener at his house before she left the office that morning and she drove directly there, parked inside the garage, and went into the house. Matthew wasn't back from the office yet, and she decided to take a quick shower before he arrived. She took her time undressing when she heard the garage door opening and a car come inside. She was expecting Matthew, but was faced with Pam.

The two women stared at each other and Silver thought that was the most embarrassing moment of her life.

Pam seemed calm and civilized as if nothing out of ordinary had happened. "I thought you two were spending the weekend in Tallahassee."

Silver stared straight into her eyes, "I thought you were spending the weekend with your lover."

"I came to pick up some things that I left here," Pam said.

"I'll wait in the other room until you finish." Silver went into the guest bedroom. She could not believe that they were so civilized about such a matter. Inside she shivered, feeling terrible about the situation.

Silver waited until Pam was gone, then took her bag and left the house. Silver stopped to see Matthew at the office and told him about the incident and returned home. She felt sick, and didn't want to go back to Matthew's house. She wanted to be alone and think about what had happened.

Later, she figured out that Matthew and Pam had a talk and Pam finally decided to leave. At least now there were no more lies, no more compromises.

CHAPTER 24

The Wild Waters

Silver had to be in Ocala for an early-morning meeting with the Marion County officials to go over a project. The meeting was scheduled for 9:00 a.m. that morning and Silver anticipated it would last, at the most, one hour. She drove to Ocala by herself the night before. She and Matthew talked about him taking the next day off from work and meeting Silver at Ocala's Wild Waters Park for the day. Matthew was to drive over in the morning and go directly to the park, and Silver would join him there after the meeting.

Silver kept the meeting informative, but brief. She responded competently to all the county officials' questions about the project. She wore an elegant silk suit.

When the meeting was over, she went back to her hotel room, changed into her bathing suit, pulled on a tee shirt and shorts, checked out of the hotel, and hurried to the Wild Waters Park to meet Matthew.

It was a gorgeous spring day, the sun already high.

Silver parked her car just outside the park's wrought iron gate, and stayed there looking for Matthew. Immediately she saw him on the other side of the fence. He did not see her. He was like an overgrown boy with his huge inflated orange tube. He climbed the steep stairs up to the top of the flume and then slid down on the orange tube, splashing in the pool at the toe of the flume. He picked up his tube and climbed back to the top of the stairs again and again, enjoying the ride with all the other kids in the park.

Silver stood still, fascinated. He could so easily transform himself into a child. She decided to join the fun. She paid the entrance fee and went inside. She called out to him. He looked startled in her direction, as if an intruder interrupted him from his favorite game.

Silver's heart squeezed painfully as she realized—she was the intruder.

Then Matthew came toward her, "You can change over there, in the restrooms."

"I don't need to, I wore my swimsuit beneath my tee shirt. Where did you leave your bag?"

"Over there, on one of those chairs."

"I won't be long," Silver went and put her things into Matthew's big bag and returned to join him.

They both started to ride the flumes, first the small ones and then the bigger, more dangerous ones. Matthew challenged Silver, showing her how to lie on her back down on the tube and ride down at maximum speed with her hands stretched behind her head like a bullet. There were long flumes and short steep flumes, open and covered flumes, all ending in a pool of water at the bottom. Then, they went into the big pool where the big artificial waves washed over their heads.

Silver's elbows turned purple from rubbing against the edges at the flumes' sudden bends.

They rode one after the other, sometimes together, challenging the speed of each other's performance. In the early afternoon, Matthew brought a big cooler from his car with a picnic he'd prepared. They sat down under the trees at the picnic tables and ate fried chicken and drank cold beer.

They had to drive home separately in their own cars. Silver followed Matthew closely and never took her eyes off him.

CHAPTER 25

The Love Making

Silver was happy with her one-bedroom apartment. It was located in a townhouse. On the first floor there was a living room and a small kitchen and upstairs was the bedroom and the bathroom. The apartment was white and clean, and she arranged it tastefully with the few possessions she brought with her from her country and the spare furniture she'd brought at garage sales around town.

Her hobby was reading; she consumed everything and any-thing that fell into her hands, but she especially loved novels. She immersed herself in the dream-like worlds of fiction, forgetting her daily worries and reality. Reading was a great way of relaxing. Every evening, Silver read for an hour or two tucked away in her bed. One night after she went to sleep, Matthew showed up at her apartment door. This time Silver understood immediately that he hadn't come to take her for a motorcycle ride, or any other rides. This time he intended to stay. Silver thought she was ready. She was not afraid of Matthew. He was her best friend. She also knew she loved him. Matthew went downstairs and prepared drinks for both of them and returned to the bedroom.

Taking off her nightgown, he started to touch Silver slowly and tenderly.

He caressed her body in an unhurried fashion. He took his time to fully arouse her before he undressed in front of her. Silver had never seen a naked man before, but Matthew was so beautiful, there was nothing to be scared or afraid of.

Then he started caressing her more: her breasts, her stomach, and then the hidden place between her legs.

He never hurried anything, as if time stood still and the two of them were all that existed. He lowered himself over her and touched her in the most intimate and beautiful way, teaching her not be ashamed of her body, that sex was the most beautiful act that could happen between two people, that she was beautiful, that he loved and cherished every part of her. He talked to her while caressing her with his hands, his mouth, and his words.

He did not demand anything from her. He only gave love and pleasure.

He probed her with his fingers. Silver assured him she was ready. Very carefully he entered her. The pain lasted only a minute and was forgotten in the midst of passion.

He stayed the night with her and awakened in the morning to again teach her the ways of love. To him, love was a natural thing. There were no inhibitions about his lovemaking, and he taught Silver to feel the same freedom. He taught her to love the fact she was a woman and not to be afraid of showing passion or giving and receiving love.

It was the greatest gift Matthew had to give her: love for herself.

CHAPTER 26

The Viskaya Villa

That week, Matthew was scheduled to go to a workshop in Dade County. Silver took several days off from the office to go with him. She had heard and read so much about Miami, she wanted to visit. They would share a hotel room, which the firm was paying for, and Matthew would take his car for the trip.

They left early in the morning. It was more than three hundred miles to Miami. They were to spend the night in Ft. Lauderdale with Frank, Matthew's best friend.

Somehow, Silver got the feeling that the meeting with Frank was very important, that the impression she made on Frank would weigh on Matthew's mind. Frank and Matthew went a long way back, since their college days.

On the drive, they drank Pepsi laced with Appleton rum, which Matthew liked very much and kept in the cooler in the trunk. They sat close together, drinking, singing along with the car radio, and not being able to keep their hands from constantly touching each other. They were in a big hurry to get to Ft. Lauderdale before

5:00 p.m. They knew Frank and his wife would be back from work by that time. If they arrived sooner, they would have the house all to themselves and a little privacy before his friend came back home.

Matthew knew where his friend kept the house key, and they were both getting aroused by their continuous touching. They just had to make it before 5:00 p.m.

They arrived at Frank's house a little bit before five and started to grab and tear each other's clothes with an intense urgency. Matthew undressed first when the downstairs front door opened, and they could hear Frank's voice.

Silver still had her clothes on and Matthew dashed for the bathroom, carrying his clothes with him. At the moment of Frank's arrival, Matthew and Silver were in the bedroom upstairs. Silver came down the stairway and greeted Frank, explaining that Matthew had gone to the bathroom to take a shower after the trip, and she was putting her bags in the guest room. Frank and his spouse, Linda, proved to be really nice. Frank and Linda's house was a brand-new town home in a new subdivision on the outskirts of Ft. Lauderdale. They had drinks, and Silver helped Linda prepare dinner while Matthew and Frank caught up on old stories. After dinner they went to the back porch, sat on lounge chairs, and talked late into the night.

Silver and Frank's wife washed dishes and put them away. Later, Frank's wife arranged two mattresses on the first floor in two different rooms, one for Silver and the other one for Matthew and she and Frank went upstairs to their bedroom.

Silver couldn't sleep. It was too exciting; too many things were happening. She went on bare feet, without making any noise, to check on Matthew. He was neatly tucked in on his mattress in the next room, sleeping peacefully. The moon was full and the light filtered through the window curtains onto Matthew's face. Silver caressed his face and hair and kissed him lightly on his face and mouth. Finally, Matthew awakened and without a sound, went back with Silver to her room to make love to her. Later, he moved back to his own place and in the morning when Frank and his wife awakened to go to work, they found them properly sleeping each in their own rooms.

They ate a hurried breakfast and drove on to Miami.

"I noticed you and Frank last night on the porch talking long after Linda and I went to bed," Silver started the discussion, unsure of herself. Somehow, she sensed that something of importance had happened last night and it had to do with Frank and Matthew's private discussion.

"Frank mentioned that he liked you," Matthew said without commitment.

"I'm glad he did, I liked them both," Silver said, not fully convinced that Matthew was telling her the entire story.

Matthew had to attend a seminar that day. They checked into the hotel and Matthew went on to the class. Silver was left alone to enjoy the day by herself. She changed into blue jeans and tee shirt and ate breakfast at the hotel's restaurant and went to explore the town. She took the skyway from the station closest to the hotel and went downtown. She stared and marveled at all the new tall buildings. She entered the small shops lining the streets where the salesmen and saleswomen talked to her in Spanish. She bought French perfume and sexy French lingerie for herself, things she could not find in her more conservative town.

Then she took the skyway back and went to visit the Viskaya Villa, a Spanish villa built in the late 1890s with all the luxury and extravagance of the time. She admired the rooms with their high ceilings and golden moldings, the antique furniture, the indoor and outdoor gardens, the private dock and the ship anchored there, the statues and vases, the flowers. In some ways it reminded her of the house she and her family had back in Romania, the Byzantine-style home she'd left behind.

When she returned to the hotel around five o'clock, the time she thought Matthew would finish his class, she found him waiting for her. He'd cut the classes short just to be with her.

They went for a short swim in the hotel's swimming pool outside, got a drink, showered and dressed for the evening.

Silver decided to put on the dress that was made for her just before she left Romania.

The dress was custom-made by a talented seamstress who derived the design from a French journal. It had a rose- colored straight slip and on top of it was the sheerest silk voile. The bodice was narrow, fitting her body closely with flounces to enhance her bosom line.

The skirt was made up of layers of voile of different lengths. The voile was printed with yellow, red, and blue dots. It was the first time she'd wanted to wear the dress.

Her chestnut hair was shoulder-length and she wore red sandals with high heels.

Matthew decided to wear his tuxedo. They went to the hotel's restaurant. The moment they entered the room, Silver noticed all the men's heads turning toward her. If it was the dress, or the glow on her face, or the twinkle in her eyes, she did not know. Never before had she noticed people staring at her so openly. She and Matthew decided to sit next to each other at the table so that they could touch during dinner. Matthew noticed all the men stared at her, and he decided to change places, to sit in front of her, contending that he was the only one missing the best view of the evening: Silver herself.

After dinner they went for a ride along the ocean near Miami Beach. For Silver's benefit, they stopped and visited some of the most famous hotels, at least stepping inside their entrances.

Finally they chose one, and went for drinks at the upstairs bar. Silver and Matthew were the only two persons in the bar that night. There was a private reception in one of the ballrooms upstairs and a lot of very elegant men and women attending it.

"You're a lucky man," the old, stylish, bartender told Matthew.

"Why is that?" Mathew said.

"You've got yourself a young and beautiful lady," the barman said, glancing appreciatively at Silver.

"You're right, I'm very lucky, indeed," Matthew said, putting his arm around her.

CHAPTER 27

The House

"You know, I'm thinking that I should buy a house pretty soon," Silver told Matthew on their way back from Miami. "And why do you want to do that?"

"I expect my family from Romania will arrive soon." "When?"

"They received their visas to enter the United States and they've already gotten passports. As soon as they finish selling their furniture, they'll be here. I have to have a place for them. They can't live in my apartment with me."

"You could rent them an apartment next to yours."

"That might be a solution, but on my salary, I'll not be able to take care of two households. It'll be awhile before they can support themselves. My mother and father are getting old; they need a place of their own."

"It looks to me like you've figured it all out. Why do you ask me?" "I want you to go with me and look at this place Maria showed me the other day. It's a new house in a new subdivision." "If you want me to, I'll come."

Matthew drove her home.

They were coming back to reality from the dream they'd been living. She had to prepare a place for the impending arrival of her family.

For the last two years, she'd worked closely with Congressman Chappell's office in Washington and the local office in Jacksonville to obtain visas for her family. Now it was time to secure a home for them. The past weekend, she and Maria found a new frame house in a subdivision in Mandarin. It was all Silver could afford on her salary, but it was a beginning, a place for the family to live. There was a living room and a dining room combination, a spacious kitchen, and three bedrooms. Not the Byzantine palace they had back home in Romania, but it would be a roof over their heads.

Silver had contacted a real estate agent to help her find a house. All the houses the agent had found in Silver's price range were older homes, blockhouses in already dilapidated neighborhoods. This one was new and clean. It was far out, but that was something they'd have to work on after the family arrived.

"I won't recommend that you go in over your head. If you borrow more money than you can comfortably pay back on your salary, you'll in trouble," Mathew cautioned her. He was good at business affairs. He had the practical side Silver was apparently lacking.

CHAPTER 28

The Vigil

It all happened very quickly. She decided on the house in the new subdivision. The paperwork went smoothly and she became the owner of the brand-new house in a matter of days. She was ready to move in and set it up. She asked Matthew and his friend who was visiting him from Tampa, and her friend, Roger, to help with the move. She didn't have a lot to move, but her car was small and she had the bed and the tables and the sofa, and all the packages her family sent from Romania. Matthew rented a small trailer and attached it to his car, and little by little they moved her entire household.

Her mother sent oil paintings they had back home in Romania. Silver painfully and minutely refinished the frames, which had been crushed into small pieces in transit. She put up curtains and mini blinds and shopped for spare beds at the discount stores, setting up bedrooms for each member of her family.

She was almost ready when her mother called from Rome, in Italy one night late. "Hi! We're here in Rome for a ten-day stay before we come to the United States. It's beautiful here. We visited the Vatican. We wish you were here to share the beauty of everything we're visiting."

"That means you'll be here in ten days?"

"Yes. I have something to tell you, but I don't want you to start crying or wear black clothes, or anything like that."

"What? What are you talking about?" Silver suddenly felt her heart squeezed tight in her chest.

"Father died. He's not with us."

"What? When did that happen? Why didn't you tell me or write me? What happened to father?"

"He had a heart attack just before the departure. We were having the medical examinations and it was cold. We had to go on foot to the clinic and when he got home, he had the attack. Mady was home alone with him. I was at the gas station trying to buy heating fuel. It was very cold in the house. We'd run out of heating oil. The furniture was all gone and the house was cold and empty. Radu tried to call an ambulance from a pay phone. The telephone company had taken the telephone out of our house because we were moving. We had to call from friends or use pay phones on the street. So much paperwork and medical examinations. It was too much for him," Mother's voice trailed off and became a whisper.

"Why didn't you tell me?" Silver started crying.

"Listen, I don't want you to wear black clothes. Your father wouldn't have liked this."

"I'll wait for you at the airport."

Silver hung up the phone and for a minute she felt totally lost, devastated. She'd prepared her mother and father's bedroom already. She'd bought a double bed for them. She made all those preparations, the house and all, with her father in mind. It was her way of showing him how much she loved him.

That's why she'd heard the stray dog howling all night few days ago. It was her father's soul visiting her. She knew it. She would not be able to get through the night alone. She called Matthew and asked him to spend the night with her.

"Hi! It's me. My father died. They just told me, now. I want you here with me tonight."

"I can't come tonight. There is nothing to be afraid of. If anything, you should welcome his spirit's visit."

"Please, I'm begging you to come over. I won't be able to survive this."

"Yes, you will. Calm down. I can't come over. Good night." She could not believe he wasn't going to come.

She called Maria, dressed, and went over to her house. By the time she arrived there, Maria had called Peggy and Melly, their Spanish friend, and they stayed up all night talking and helping her with a lighted candle on the coffee table between them, keeping vigil.

CHAPTER 29

The Prayer

The next day, Monday, she went to work. She couldn't talk to anybody. She was so hurt, so deeply affected by the news of her father's death that she couldn't talk to anyone.

"Silver, please call Father Costopuolos at the church and talk to him," Maria urged her. "It'll help."

Finally by the next day, when she couldn't bear the pain any longer, she called the church and asked for the priest. He came on the line right away.

"Father, my father died back in Romania. He's not coming, and I was waiting for him along with the others."

"He's with God now! Let him go. I'll pray for his soul. When you can, when your family is here, then you can have a service for your father at the church."

"I can't do it now. I can't talk to anyone about the loss. It's too painful."

"I understand. When you're ready. I'll pray for him and for you."

After she hung up, she calmed down as if touched by an angel. The pain eased to the point that she could live with it.

She couldn't help but think that Maria and her friends were there for her in her time of need, but Matthew was not.

CHAPTER 30

The Family's Arrival

The big day came. Her family was to arrive that afternoon at the Jacksonville airport. She got the flight number and the arrival time, notified all her friends, Maria and Peggy and Melly and got them ready to go with her to the airport, and Matthew too.

"Are you sure you don't want the flowers and the balloons and maybe the media at the airport, too?" Maria had asked her a few days before the big day.

"No, my family wouldn't like that! They're mourning my father's death and they wouldn't appreciate it. I'll buy mother a bouquet of fresh cut flowers. If you'll bring your car to the airport, they have a lot of luggage with them. I'll go with Matthew in his car, but probably we'll need more than one car to haul everything."

"Melly could take her car. It's bigger than mine."

"I prepared a party at the house for after we arrive home. I cooked <u>tiropita</u> and Russian salad and a chocolate cake. I'll have it ready when we get home."

133

At the airport, Silver and Matthew waited at the terminal to meet her family, while Maria and Melly and Peggy went downstairs by the carousels to receive and carry the luggage to the cars. Or perhaps it was their way of giving Silver and her family some time to be alone.

She waited with Matthew on the chairs next to the arrival door. Passengers started to come out of the airplane. "I don't know. I have this heavy feeling in my heart all of sudden. I don't know why," Silver said.

"That's nonsense. You're overly excited. That's all."

"Mother, Radu, Mady—here I am! Welcome to America," Silver cried and ran to embrace her mother and brother and sister. It had been five years since Silver had left Romania and her family. Her Mother looked so frail, and all of them, Radu especially, were marked by the sadness of the loss of their father.

"Mother, this is my friend and colleague Matthew." She noticed Matthew stayed off to the side, as if he were a stranger looking from the outside at a family reunion.

"Nice to meet you," her mother said in Romanian. Her mother did not speak English. Silver had to translate.

"Mother, here are some flowers for you. Let's go downstairs and get the luggage from the carousel and meet my other friends."

"I'll take some pictures of you all here," Matthew said. "It'll make a good memory."

They all went downstairs and met Maria, Peggy, and Melly. "Mother, this is Maria. She's Greek and you can speak Greek to her." "Ooh. So nice to meet you, Maria. Silver has told and written so much about you. Finally, I can speak to someone."

They went home, Silver with Matthew and her mother, and the others in Melly and Peggy's car. A piece of luggage was lost, but they were assured the airline would deliver it to the house the next day.

It was an hour's drive to her home on the south side of town. Outside it was dark, and her mother looked frightened at the dark, empty roads. "That's the house?" her mother asked, looking incredulous at the small frame house surrounded by woods.

"That's the house," Silver responded. For the first time she saw the house through her mother's eyes, and knew it looked pitiful compared to the monumental structures of urban Europe.

"Mother, please come inside. I have prepared a party for your arrival.

I'll set up the table and bring out the food in a minute."

Everyone found a place at the round table and Silver started bringing out the food she'd prepared a week in advance.

She noticed again that Matthew remained outside the circle. He did not belong, nor did he have any desire to belong.

What happened over the next few months was a blur of frenzied activities for Silver. There were forms to complete for her mother and brother and sister, English classes to attend, driving tests to be passed, jobs to be found. A lot of things. Silver's family needed her at home and Matthew was left on the outside. He made no effort to become a part of the family, nor did he offer to help the family to get established. Silver was not available to him to play and attend his every whim and he felt betrayed. They were pulling apart and Silver's heart was aching.

Finally, she learned that he was back with Pam. She was his safety net as her family was hers.

"You're back with Pam," Silver confronted Matthew one afternoon at work.

"She understands me and doesn't try to change me," Matthew said. "But, do you love her?"

"It's survival. It's that simple. She and I go a long way back. She puts up with me the way I am. She's not as demanding as you are."

"Is that all there was to our love?"

"You have your family now. You're not alone any longer." "Yes, I have my family, thanks God."

When she got home that evening, she went straight to her bedroom and shut the door. There, in the privacy of her room, she started to cry as she felt her heart had been crushed and the pain was unbearable.

"Mother, go and talk to her, now! She needs to be with somebody. She'll not be able to get through this alone," Silver overheard Radu's concerned voice outside her bedroom door.

-The End-

www.ingramcontent.com/pod-product-compliance
Lightning Source LLC
Chambersburg PA
CBHW071956150726
47999CB00001B/459